Anti-Inflammatory Diet Cookbook For Two

2 Books in 1| A Meal Plan for Healthy Couples | Complete Guide to transform your Bodies and Reduce Inflammation | 200 Quick and Easy Recipes to Weight Loss and Eat Healthy

(Collector's Edition)

By Annette Baker

Table of Contents

Anti-Inflammatory Diet Cookbook For Women

Anti-Inflammatory Diet Cookbook For Men

Anti-Inflammatory Diet Cookbook For Women

A Step-by-step Guide to Weight Loss With Delicious and Affordable Recipes | A No-Stress Meal Plan to Fight Inflammation and Prevent Breast Cancer

By Annette Baker

Chapter 1: Introduction

Inflammation is a problem that affects a large part of the world's population, mainly women. Women are the ones who suffer most from inflammation due to their metabolism, hormonal changes during the menstrual cycle, but it can also be a consequence of a gynecological infection. Therefore, this diet allows you to avoid the discomfort caused by inflammation and prevent gynecological diseases such as breast cancer.

In this cookbook I will teach you how to get rid of your swollen belly and feel lighter with a proper diet and delicious recipes that will make your anti-inflammatory diet a lifestyle. Also remember to see your gynecologist at least once a year to rule out inflammation due to gynecological infections.

What does the anti-inflammatory diet consist of?

The anti-inflammatory diet consists of naturally reducing inflammation. Its main differentiator is that it includes foods with a nutritional contribution and components with proven anti-inflammatory effect.

Besides following the indications of the recipes, it is important to eat calmly, chewing the food conscientiously, taking the necessary time for each bite. Try to walk for at least 10 minutes after eating. By following this diet and these tips you will get rid of the swollen belly, and acquire habits that will improve your life and your figure, to look and feel like a Diva.

What foods can I eat on the anti-inflammatory diet?

This diet stars natural, non-processed foods such as vegetables, tubers, fruits and vegetables, oily fish, eggs, mushrooms, coconut and olive oil, dark chocolate, coffee, seaweed and spices.

Although it includes fruits and vegetables, this diet advises to avoid foods that can cause inflammation such as lettuce, sodas or raw vegetables. Cooked vegetables are better digested, and legumes are easier to digest with 24 hours soaking. Always prefer nuts and not cereals.

Now you know the basics of the anti-inflammatory diet, so get ready to enjoy a better quality of life, wear a tight dress or those stretch jeans without fear.
Here you will find recipes that you can make easily and with the tranquility of having the right ingredients and portions to say "bye to inflammation".

Breakfast Recipes

1) Gluten Free Crepes

Preparation Time: **Cooking Time: [30 minutes]**   **Servings: [10]**

Ingredients:

- Option 1
- Making crepes using gluten-free and gum-free waffle and pancake mix
- 3 tablespoons sugar
- 1 1/2 cups gluten-free pancake mix
- 1 cup of cold water
- 2 eggs
- 2 tablespoons butter, melted

- Option 2
- Making crepes using your favorite gluten-free and gum-free flour blend:
- 2 tablespoons butter, melted
- 3 tablespoons sugar
- 1 cup of cold water
- 2 tablespoons cold water
- 2 eggs
- 1 1/2 cups gluten-free flour
- 1/2 tsp gluten-free baking powder or mix baking soda and cream of tartar in equal parts
- 1/2 tsp vanilla extract

Directions:

⇒ In a large bowl, mix all crepe ingredients, and whisk the mixture until the lumps dissolve. Allow/let the mixture sit at room temperature for some 15 minutes. After 15 minutes, it will become thickened.

⇒ Heat the frying pan to very hot, spray it with oil spray and pour a small amount of batter into the frying pan using a soup spoon or 1/4 measuring cup as you roll the pan from side-side.

⇒ Allow this thin layer of crepe batter to cook for 1, 2, or 3 minutes, then turn the crepe to the other side, then let it cook for another minute.

Nutrition: [Calories 100Carbs: 14gFat: 4gProtein: 3g]

2) Scrambled Eggs With Mushrooms And Spinach

Preparation Time: **Cooking Time:**   **Servings:[1]**

Ingredients:

- 2 egg whites
- 1 slice whole wheat toast
- ½ c. sliced fresh mushrooms
- 2 tbsps. Shredded fat-free American cheese

- Pepper
- 1 tsp. olive oil
- 1 c. chopped fresh spinach
- 1 whole egg

Directions:

⇒ On medium-high fire, place a nonstick fry pan and add oil. Swirl oil to cover pan and heat for a minute.

⇒ Add spinach and mushrooms. Sauté until spinach is wilted, around 2-3 minutes.

⇒ Meanwhile, in a bowl whisk well egg, egg whites, and cheese. Season with pepper.

⇒ Pour egg mixture into pan and scramble until eggs are cooked through, around 3-4 minutes.

⇒ Serve and enjoy with a piece of whole wheat toast.

Nutrition: [Calories: 290.6, Fat:11.8 g, Carbs:21.8 g, Protein:24.3 g, Sugars:1.4 g, Sodium:1000 mg]

3) Savory Breakfast Pancakes

Preparation Time: **Cooking Time: [6 minutes]**   **Servings:[4]**

Ingredients:

- ½ cup almond flour
- ½ cup tapioca flour
- 1 cup coconut milk
- ½ teaspoon chili powder
- ¼ teaspoon turmeric powder

- ½ red onion, chopped
- 1 handful cilantro leaves, chopped
- ½ inch ginger, grated
- 1 teaspoon salt
- ¼ teaspoon ground black pepper

Directions:

⇒ In a mixing bowl, mix all ingredients until well-combined.

⇒ Heat a pan on low medium heat and grease with oil.

⇒ Pour ¼ cup of batter onto the pan and spread the mixture to create a pancake.

⇒ Fry for 3 minutes per side.

⇒ Repeat until the batter is done.

Nutrition: [Calories 108Total Fat 2gSaturated Fat 1gTotal Carbs 20gNet Carbs 19.5gProtein 2gSugar: 4gFiber: 0.5gSodium: 37mgPotassium 95mg]

4) Maple Mocha Frappe

Preparation Time: **Cooking Time:**   **Servings:[2]**

Ingredients:

- 1 tbsp. unsweetened cocoa powder
- ½ c. low-fat milk
- 2 tbsps. Pure maple syrup

- ½ c. brewed coffee
- 1 small ripe banana
- 1 c. low-fat vanilla yogurt

Directions:

⇒ Place the banana in a blender or food processor and purée.

⇒ Add the remaining ingredients and pulse until smooth and creamy.

⇒ Serve immediately.

Nutrition: [Calories: 206, Fat:2 g, Carbs:38 g, Protein:6 g, Sugars:17 g, Sodium:65 mg]

5) Chocolaty Almond Flour And Peanut Butter Muffins

Preparation Time: **Cooking Time: [25 minutes]**   **Servings:[6]**

Ingredients:

- 1 cup almond flour
- 1 tsp baking powder
- 1/8 tsp salt
- ½ cup erythritol

- 1/3 cup almond milk, unsweetened
- 2 organic eggs
- 1/3 cup peanut butter, unsweetened
- 2 tbsp cocoa nibs

Directions:

⇒ Switch on the oven, then set its temperature to 350°F and let it preheat.

⇒ Meanwhile, place flour in a bowl, add baking powder, salt, and erythritol and stir until mixed.

⇒ Then pour in milk, add eggs and peanut butter, whisk until incorporated and then fold in cocoa nibs.

⇒ Take a six cups muffin tray, line the cups with muffin liner, fill them evenly with prepared batter and bake for 25 minutes until muffins have cooked through and nicely browned.

⇒ When done, transfer muffins to a wire rack to cool completely, then wrap each muffin with a foil and store in the refrigerator for up to five days.

⇒ Serve the muffins when ready to eat.

Nutrition: [Calories 265, Total Fat 20.5g, Total Carbs 2g, Protein 7.5g]

6) Cauliflower Waffles With Cheesy And Thyme

Preparation Time: **Cooking Time:[15 Minutes]**   **Servings:[2]**

Ingredients:

- ½ cup shredded mozzarella cheese
- ¼ cup grated parmesan cheese
- ¼ large head of cauliflower
- ½ cup collard greens
- 1 large organic egg
- 1 stalk of green onion

- ½ tbsp olive oil
- ½ tsp garlic powder
- ¼ tsp salt
- ½ tbsp sesame seed
- 1 tsp fresh thyme, chopped
- ¼ tsp cracked black pepper

Directions:

⇒ Put cauliflower, in a food processor, add spring onion, collard greens, and thyme and then pulse for 2 to 3 minutes until smooth.

⇒ Tip the mixture in a bowl, add remaining ingredients and stir until mixed.

⇒ Switch on the waffle iron, grease it with oil and when hot, ladle half of the prepared batter in it, shut with lid, and cook until nicely brown and firm.

⇒ When done, transfer waffle to a plate and cook another waffle in the same manner by using the remaining batter.

⇒ Serve straight away.

Nutrition: [Calories 144, Total Carbs 8.5, Total Fat 9.4g, Protein 9.3g, Sugar 3g, Sodium 435mg]

7) Sweet Corn Muffins

Preparation Time: **Cooking Time:**   **Servings:[1]**

Ingredients:

- 1 tbsp. sodium-free baking powder
- ¾ c. nondairy milk
- 1 tsp. pure vanilla extract
- ½ c. sugar

- 1 c. white whole-wheat flour
- 1 c. cornmeal
- ½ c. canola oil

Directions:

⇒ Preheat the oven to 400°F. Line a 12-muffin tin with paper liners and set aside.

⇒ Place the cornmeal, flour, sugar, and baking powder into a mixing bowl and whisk well to combine.

⇒ Add the nondairy milk, oil, and vanilla and stir just until combined.

⇒ Divide the batter evenly between the muffin cups. Place muffin tin on middle rack in the oven and bake for 15 minutes.

⇒ Remove from oven and place on a wire rack to cool.

Nutrition: [Calories: 203, Fat:9 g, Carbs:26 g, Protein:3 g, Sugars:9.5 g, Sodium:255 mg]

8) Fresh & Fruity Perky Parfait

Preparation Time: **Cooking Time:[0 minutes]**   **Servings:[2]**

Ingredients:

- ½-cup fresh raspberries
- A pinch of cinnamon
- 1-tsp maple syrup

- 2-Tbsps chia seeds
- 16-oz. plain yogurt
- Fresh fruit: sliced blackberries, nectarines, or strawberries

Directions:

⇒ By using a fork, mash the raspberries in a mixing bowl until achieving a jam-like consistency. Add the cinnamon, syrup, and chia seeds. Continue mashing until incorporating all the ingredients. Set aside.

⇒ In two serving glasses, alternate layers of yogurt and the mixture. Garnish with fresh fruit slices.

Nutrition: [Calories 315Fat: 8.7gProtein: 19.6gSodium: 164mgTotal Carbs: 45.8gDietary Fiber: 6.5g]

9) Cream Cheese Salmon Toast

Preparation Time: **Cooking Time:**[2 mnutes]   **Servings:**[2]

Ingredients:

- Whole grain or rye toast, two slices
- Red onion, chopped fine, two tablespoons
- Cream cheese, low fat, two tablespoons

- Basil flakes, one half teaspoon
- Arugula or spinach, chopped, one half cup
- Smoked salmon, two ounces

Directions:

⇒ Toast the wheat bread. Mix cream cheese and basil and spread this mixture on the toast.

⇒ Add salmon, arugula, and onion.

Nutrition: [Calories 291 fat 15.2 grams carbohydrates 17.8 gramssugar 3 grams]

10) Peaches With Honey Almond Ricotta

Preparation Time: **Cooking Time:**[0 minutes]   **Servings:**[6]

Ingredients:

Spread

- Ricotta, skim milk, one cup
- Honey, one teaspoon
- Almonds, thin slices, one half cup

- Almond extract, one quarter teaspoon

To Serve

- Peaches, sliced, one cup
- Bread, whole grain bagel or toast

Directions:

⇒ Mix the almond extract, honey, ricotta, and almonds.

⇒ Spread one tablespoon of this mix on toasted bread and cover with peaches.

Nutrition: [Calories 230 protein 9 gramsfat 8 gramscarbs grams 37fiber 3 grams sugar 34 grams]

11) Blueberry Muffins

Preparation Time: **Cooking Time:**[22-25 minutes]   **Servings:**[10]

Ingredients:

- 2½ cups almond flour
- 1 tablespoon coconut flour
- ½ tsp baking soda
- 3 tablespoons ground cinnamon, divided
- Salt, to taste
- 2 organic eggs

- ¼ cup coconut milk
- ¼ cup coconut oil
- ¼ cup maple syrup
- 1 tablespoon organic vanilla flavor
- 1 cup fresh blueberries

Directions:

⇒ Preheat the oven to 350 degrees F. Grease 10 cups of a large muffin tin.

⇒ In a big bowl, mix together flours, baking soda, 2 tablespoons of cinnamon and salt.

⇒ In another bowl, add eggs, milk, oil, maple syrup and vanilla and beat till well combined.

⇒ Add egg mixture into flour mixture and mix till well combined.

⇒ Fold in blueberries.

⇒ Place a combination into prepared muffin cups evenly.

⇒ Sprinkle with cinnamon evenly.

⇒ Bake for approximately 22-25 minutes or till a toothpick inserted within the center is released clean.

Nutrition: [Calories: 328, Fat: 11g, Carbohydrates: 29g, Fiber: 5g, Protein: 19g]

12) Blueberry Smoothie

Preparation Time: **Cooking Time:[0 minutes]**   **Servings:[1]**

Ingredients:

- 1 banana, peeled
- 2 handfuls baby spinach
- 1 tablespoon almond butter
- ½ cup blueberries

- ¼ teaspoon ground cinnamon
- 1 teaspoon maca powder
- ½ cup water
- ½ cup almond milk, unsweetened

Directions:

⇒ In your blender, mix the spinach with the banana, blueberries, almond butter, cinnamon, maca powder, water and milk.

⇒ Pulse well, pour into a glass and serve.

⇒ Enjoy!

Nutrition: [calories 341, fat 12, fiber 11, carbs 54, protein 10]

13) Kale Turmeric Scramble

Preparation Time: **Cooking Time:[10 minutes]**   **Servings:[1]**

Ingredients:

- Olive oil, two tablespoons
- Kale, shredded, one half cup
- Sprouts, one half cup
- Garlic, minced, one tablespoon

- Black pepper, one quarter teaspoon
- Turmeric, ground, one tablespoon
- Eggs, two

Directions:

⇒ Beat the eggs and add in the turmeric, black pepper, and garlic. Sauté the kale into the olive oil over medium heat for five minutes, and then pour this egg batter into the pan with the kale.

⇒ Continue cooking, often stirring, until the eggs are cooked. Top with raw sprouts and serve.

Nutrition: [Calories 137 fat 8.4 grams carbs 7.9 grams fiber 4.8 grams sugar 1.8gramsprotein 13.2 grams]

14) Cheese And Sausage Casserole With Tasty Marinara

Preparation Time: **Cooking Time:[20 minutes]**   **Servings:[6]**

Ingredients:

- ½ tbsp olive oil
- ½ lb sausage
- 2.5oz marinara sauce

- 4 oz shredded parmesan cheese
- 4 oz shredded mozzarella cheese

Directions:

⇒ Switch on the oven, then set its temperature to 375°F and let it preheat.

⇒ Take a baking dish, grease it with oil, add half of the sausage in it, scramble it and spread it evenly in the bottom of the dish.

⇒ Top the sausage in the baking dish with half of each marinara sauce, parmesan, and mozzarella cheese, and then spread the remaining sausage on top.

⇒ Layer the sausage with remaining marinara sauce, parmesan, and mozzarella cheese and then bake for 20 minutes until sausage has cooked and cheeses have melted.

⇒ When done, let the casserole cool completely, then divide it evenly between six airtight containers and store in the refrigerator for up to 12 days.

⇒ When ready to eat, reheat casserole in the microwave until hot and serve.

Nutrition: [Calories 353, Total Fat 24.3g, Total Carbs 5.5g, Protein 28.4, Sugar 5g, Sodium 902mg]

15) Golden Milk Chia Pudding

Preparation Time: **Cooking Time:[0 minutes]**   **Servings:[4]**

Ingredients:

- 4 cups coconut milk
- 3 tablespoons honey
- 1 teaspoon vanilla extract
- 1 teaspoon ground turmeric
- ½ teaspoon ground cinnamon

- ½ teaspoon ground ginger
- ¾ cup coconut yogurt
- ½ cup chia seeds
- 1 cup fresh mixed berry
- ¼ cup toasted coconut chips

Directions:

⇒ In a mixing bowl, combine the coconut milk, honey, vanilla extract, turmeric, cinnamon, and ginger. Add in the coconut yogurt.

⇒ In bowls, place chia seeds, berries, and coconut chips.

⇒ Pour in the milk mixture.

⇒ Allow to chill in the fridge to set for 6 hours.

Nutrition: [Calories 337Total Fat 11gSaturated Fat 2gTotal Carbs 51gNet Carbs 49gProtein 10gSugar: 29gFiber: 2gSodium: 262mgPotassium 508mg]

16) Carrot Cake Overnight Oats

Preparation Time: **Cooking Time:[1 minute]**   **Servings:[2]**

Ingredients:

- Coconut or almond milk, one cup
- Chia seeds, one tablespoon
- Cinnamon, ground, one teaspoon
- Raisins, one half cup

- Cream cheese, low fat, two tablespoons at room temperature
- Carrot, one large peel, and shred
- Honey, two tablespoons
- Vanilla, one teaspoon

Directions:

⇒ Mix all of the listed items and store them in a safe refrigerator container overnight. Eat cold in the morning.

⇒ If you choose to warm this, just microwave for one minute and stir well before eating.

Nutrition: [Calories 340 sugar 32 grams protein 8 grams fat 4 grams fiber 9 grams carbs 70 grams]

17) Honey Pancakes

Preparation Time: **Cooking Time:[5 minutes]**   **Servings:[2]**

Ingredients:

- ½ cup almond flour
- 2 tablespoons coconut flour
- 1 tablespoon ground flaxseeds
- ¼ tsp baking soda
- ½ tablespoon ground ginger
- ½ tablespoon ground nutmeg
- ½ tablespoon ground cinnamon

- ½ teaspoon ground cloves
- Pinch of salt
- 2 tablespoons organic honey
- ¾ cup organic egg whites
- ½ teaspoon organic vanilla extract
- Coconut oil, as required

Directions:

⇒ In a big bowl, mix together flours, flax seeds, baking soda, spices and salt.

⇒ In another bowl, add honey, egg whites and vanilla and beat till well combined.

⇒ Add egg mixture into flour mixture and mix till well combined.

⇒ Lightly, grease a big nonstick skillet with oil and heat on medium-low heat.

⇒ Add about ¼ cup of mixture and tilt the pan to spread it evenly inside skillet.

⇒ Cook for about 3-4 minutes.

⇒ Carefully, customize the side and cook approximately 1 minute more.

⇒ Repeat with the remaining mixture.

⇒ Serve along with your desired topping.

Nutrition: [Calories: 291, Fat: 8g, Carbohydrates: 26g, Fiber: 4g, Protein: 23g]

Lunch & Dinner Recipes

18) Sweet Potato Soup

Preparation Time: **Cooking Time:[15 minutes]**   **Servings:[6]**

Ingredients:

- 2 tablespoons of olive oil
- 1 medium onion, chopped
- 1 can of green chilies
- 1 teaspoon of ground cumin
- 1 teaspoon of ground ginger

- 1 teaspoon of sea salt
- 4 cups of sweet potatoes, peeled and chopped
- 4 cups of organic, low-sodium vegetable broth
- 2 tablespoons of fresh cilantro, minced
- 6 tablespoons of Greek yogurt

Directions:

⇒ Heat-up the olive oil over medium heat in a large soup pot. Add in the onion, and sauté until soft. Add in the green chilies and seasonings, and cook for 2 minutes.

⇒ Stir in the sweet potatoes and vegetable broth, and bring to a boil.

⇒ Simmer within 15 minutes.

⇒ Stir in the minced cilantro.

⇒ Blend half of the soup until smooth. Put it back to the pot with the remaining soup.

⇒ Season with extra sea salt if desired, and top with a dollop of Greek yogurt.

Nutrition: [Total Carbohydrates 33g Dietary Fiber: 5g Protein: 6g Total Fat: 5g Calories: 192]

19) Broccolini With Almonds

Preparation Time: **Cooking Time:[5 minutes]**   **Servings:[6]**

Ingredients:

- 1 fresh red chili, deseeded and finely chopped
- 2 bunches of broccolini, trimmed
- 1 tablespoon extra-virgin olive oil
- 2 garlic cloves, thinly sliced

- 1/4 cup natural almonds, coarsely chopped
- 2 teaspoons lemon rind, finely grated
- 4 anchovies in oil, chopped
- A squeeze of fresh lemon juice

Directions:

⇒ Preheat some oil in a pan. Add 2 teaspoons of lemon rind, drained anchovies, finely chopped chili, and thinly sliced gloves. Cook for about 30 seconds, with constant stirring.

⇒ Add 1/4 cup coarsely chopped almonds and cook for a minute. Turn the heat off and add lemon juice on top.

⇒ Place the steamer basket over a pan with simmering water. Add broccolini to a basket and cover it.

⇒ Cook until tender-crisp, for about 3-4 minutes. Drain and then transfer to the serving platter.

⇒ Top with almond mixture and enjoy!

Nutrition: [414 calories 6.6 g fat 1.6 g total carbs 5.4 g protein]

20) Clean Eating Egg Salad

Preparation Time: **Cooking Time:[0 Minutes]**   **Servings:2**

Ingredients:

- 6 organic pasture-raised eggs, hard-boiled
- 1 avocado
- ¼ cup of Greek yogurt
- 2 tablespoons of olive oil mayonnaise

- 1 teaspoon of fresh dill
- Sea salt to taste
- Lettuce for serving

Directions:

⇒ Mash the hard-boiled eggs and avocado together.

⇒ Add in the Greek yogurt, olive oil mayonnaise, and fresh dill.

⇒ Season with sea salt. Serve on a bed of lettuce.

Nutrition: [Total Carbohydrates 18g Dietary Fiber: 10g Protein: 23g Total Fat: 38g Calories: 486]

21) White Bean Chili

Preparation Time: **Cooking Time:[20 minutes]**   **Servings:[4]**

Ingredients:

- ¼ cup extra-virgin olive oil
- 2 small onions, cut into ¼-inch dice
- 2 celery stalks, thinly sliced
- 2 small carrots, peeled and thinly sliced
- 2 garlic cloves, minced
- 2 teaspoons ground cumin
- 1½ teaspoons dried oregano

- 1 teaspoon salt
- ¼ teaspoon freshly ground black pepper
- 3 cups vegetable broth
- 1 (15½-ounce) can white beans, drained and rinsed
- ¼ finely chopped fresh flat-leaf parsley
- 2 teaspoons grated or minced lemon zest

Directions:

⇒ Heat-up the oil over high heat in a Dutch oven.

⇒ Add the onions, celery, carrots, and garlic and sauté until softened, 5 to 8 minutes.

⇒ Add the cumin, oregano, salt, and pepper and sauté to toast the spices, about 1 minute.

⇒ Put the broth and boil.

⇒ Simmer, add the beans, and cook, partially covered and occasionally stirring, for 5 minutes to develop the flavors.

⇒ Mix in the parsley and lemon zest and serve.

Nutrition: [Calories 300 Total Fat: 15g Total Carbohydrates: 32g Sugar: 4g Fiber: 12gProtein: 12gSodium: 1183mg]

22) Lemon Tuna

Preparation Time: **Cooking Time:[18 minutes]**   **Servings:[4]**

Ingredients:

- 4 tuna steaks
- 1 tablespoon olive oil
- ½ teaspoon smoked paprika
- ¼ teaspoon black peppercorns, crushed

- Juice of 1 lemon
- 4 scallions, chopped
- 1 tablespoon chives, chopped

Directions:

⇒ Heat up a pan with the oil over medium-high heat, add the scallions and sauté for 2 minutes.

⇒ Add the tuna steaks and sear them for 2 minutes on each side.

⇒ Add the remaining ingredients, toss gently, introduce the pan in the oven and bake at 360 degrees F for 12 minutes.

⇒ Divide everything between plates and serve for lunch.

Nutrition: [calories 324, fat 1, fiber 2, carbs 17, protein 22]

23) Tilapia With Asparagus And Acorn Squash

Preparation Time: **Cooking Time:[30 minutes]**   **Servings:[4]**

Ingredients:

- 2 tablespoons extra-virgin olive oil
- 1 medium acorn squash, seeded and thinly sliced or in wedges
- 1-pound asparagus, trimmed of woody ends and cut into 2-inch pieces
- 1 large shallot, thinly sliced

- 1-pound tilapia fillets
- ½ cup white wine
- 1 tablespoon chopped fresh flat-leaf parsley
- 1 teaspoon salt
- ¼ teaspoon freshly ground black pepper

Directions:

⇒ Preheat the oven to 400°F. Grease the baking sheet with the oil.

⇒ Arrange the squash, asparagus, and shallot in a single layer on the baking sheet. Roast within 8 to 10 minutes.

⇒ Put the tilapia, and add the wine.

⇒ Sprinkle with the parsley, salt, and pepper.

⇒ Roast within 15 minutes. Remove, then let rest for 5 minutes, and serve.

Nutrition: [Calories 246 Total Fat: 8g Total Carbohydrates: 17g Sugar: 2g Fiber: 4g Protein: 25g Sodium: 639mg]

24) Bake Chicken Top-up With Olives, Tomatoes, And Basil

Preparation Time: **Cooking Time:** 45 minutes   **Servings:** 4

Ingredients:

- 8 Chicken thighs
- Small Italian tomatoes
- 1tbsp Black pepper & salt
- 1tbsp Olive oil
- 15 Basil leaves (large)
- Small black olives
- 1-2 Fresh red chili flakes

Directions:

⇒ Marinate chicken pieces with all spices & olive oil and leave it for some time.

⇒ Assemble chicken pieces in a rimmed pan with top-up with tomatoes, basil leaves, olives, and chili flakes.

⇒ Bake this chicken in an already preheated oven (at 220C) for 40 minutes.

⇒ Bake until the chicken is tender, tomatoes, basil, and olives are cooked.

⇒ Garnish it with fresh parsley and lemon zest.

Nutrition: [Calories 304Carbs: 18gFat: 7gProtein: 41g]

25) Ratatouille

Preparation Time: **Cooking Time:** [25 minutes]   **Servings:** [8]

Ingredients:

- 1 Zucchini, medium & diced
- 3 tbsp. Extra Virgin Olive Oil
- 2 Bell Pepper, diced
- 1 Yellow Squash, medium & diced
- 1 Onion, large & diced
- 28 oz. Whole Tomatoes, peeled
- 1 Eggplant, medium & diced with skin on
- Salt & Pepper, as needed
- 4 Thyme Sprigs, fresh
- 5 Garlic cloves, chopped

Directions:

⇒ To start with, heat a large sauté pan over medium-high heat.

⇒ Once hot, spoon in the oil, onion, and garlic to it.

⇒ Sauté the onion mixture for 3 to 5 minutes or until softened.

⇒ Next, stir in the eggplant, pepper, thyme, and salt to the pan. Mix well.

⇒ Now, cook for further 5 minutes or until the eggplant becomes softened.

⇒ Then, add zucchini, bell peppers, and squash to the pan and continue cooking for another 5 minutes. Then, stir in the tomatoes and mix well.

⇒ Once everything is added, give a good stir until everything comes together. Allow it to simmer for 15 minutes.

⇒ Finally, check for seasoning and spoon in more salt and pepper if needed.

⇒ Garnish with parsley and ground black pepper.

Nutrition: [Calories: 103KcalProteins: 2gCarbohydrates: 12gFat: 5g]

26) Sheet Pan Steak With Brussels Sprouts And Red Wine

Preparation Time: **Cooking Time:** [20 minutes]   **Servings:** [4]

Ingredients:

- 1-pound rib-eye steak
- 1 teaspoon salt
- ¼ teaspoon freshly ground black pepper
- 1 tablespoon unsalted butter
- ½ red onion, minced
- 8 ounces Brussels sprouts, trimmed and quartered
- 1 cup red wine
- Juice of ½ lemon

Directions:

⇒ Preheat the broiler on high.

⇒ Massage the steak with the salt and pepper on a large rimmed baking sheet. Broil until browned, 2 to 3 minutes per side.

⇒ Turn off and heat-up the oven to 400°F.

⇒ Put the steak on one side of the baking sheet and add the butter, onion, Brussels sprouts, and wine to the other side.

⇒ Roast within 8 minutes. Remove, and let rest for 5 minutes.

⇒ Sprinkle with the lemon juice and serve.

Nutrition: [Calories 416 Total Fat: 27g Total Carbohydrates: 8g Sugar: 2g Fiber: 3g Protein: 22g Sodium: 636mg]

27) Chicken Meatball Soup

Preparation Time: **Cooking Time:[30 minutes]**   **Servings:[4]**

Ingredients:

- 2 pounds chicken breast, skinless, boneless and minced
- 2 tablespoons cilantro, chopped
- 2 eggs, whisked
- 1 garlic clove, minced
- ¼ cup green onions, chopped
- 1 yellow onion, chopped
- 1 carrot, sliced
- 1 tablespoon olive oil
- 5 cups chicken stock
- 1 tablespoon parsley, chopped
- A pinch of salt and black pepper

Directions:

⇒ In a bowl, combine the meat with the eggs and the other ingredients except the oil, yellow onion, stock and the parsley, stir and shape medium meatballs out of this mix.

⇒ Heat up a pot with the oil over medium heat, add the yellow onion and the meatballs and brown for 5 minutes.

⇒ Add the remaining ingredients, toss, bring to a simmer and cook over medium heat for 25 minutes more.

⇒ Ladle the soup into bowls and serve.

Nutrition: [calories 200, fat 2, fiber 2, carbs 14, protein 12]

28) Cabbage Orange Salad With Citrusy Vinaigrette

Preparation Time: **Cooking Time:[0 minutes]**   **Servings:[8]**

Ingredients:

- 1 teaspoon orange zest, grated
- 2 tablespoons vegetable stock, reduced-sodium
- 1 teaspoon each cider vinegar
- 4 cups red cabbage, shredded
- 1 teaspoon lemon juice
- 1 fennel bulb, sliced thinly
- 1 teaspoon balsamic vinegar
- 1 teaspoon raspberry vinegar
- 2 tablespoons of fresh orange juice
- 2 oranges, peeled, cut into pieces
- 1 tablespoon of honey
- 1/4 teaspoon of salt
- Freshly ground pepper
- 4 teaspoons of olive oil

Directions:

⇒ Put lemon juice, orange zest, cider vinegar, salt and pepper, broth, oil, honey, orange juice, balsamic vinegar, and raspberry in a bowl and whisk.

⇒ Extract the oranges, fennel, and cabbage. Toss to coat.

Nutrition: [Calories 70Carbs: 14gFat: 0gProtein: 1g]

29) Tempeh And Root Vegetable Bake

Preparation Time: **Cooking Time: [30 minutes]**   **Servings:[4]**

Ingredients:

- 1 tablespoon extra-virgin olive oil
- 1 large sweet potato, dice
- 2 carrots, thinly sliced
- 1 fennel bulb, trimmed and cut into ¼-inch dice
- 2 teaspoons minced fresh ginger
- 1 garlic clove, minced
- 12 ounces tempeh, cut into ½-inch dice
- ½ cup vegetable broth
- 1 tablespoon gluten-free tamari or soy sauce
- 2 scallions, thinly sliced

Directions:

⇒ Preheat the oven to 400°F. Grease a baking sheet with the oil.

⇒ Arrange the sweet potato, carrots, fennel, ginger, and garlic in a single layer on the baking sheet.

⇒ Bake until the vegetables have softened, about 15 minutes.

⇒ Add the tempeh, broth, and tamari.

⇒ Bake again until the tempeh is heated through and lightly browned 10 to 15 minutes.

⇒ Add the scallions, mix well, and serve.

Nutrition: [Calories 276 Total Fat: 13g Total Carbohydrates: 26g Sugar: 5g Fiber: 4g Protein: 19g Sodium: 397mg]

30) Green Soup

Preparation Time: **Cooking Time:[5 minutes]**   **Servings:[2]**

Ingredients:

- 1 cup Water
- 1 cup Spinach, fresh & packed
- ½ of 1 Lemon, peeled
- 1 Zucchini, small & chopped
- 2 tbsp. Parsley, fresh & chopped
- 1 Celery Stalk, chopped

- Sea Salt & Black Pepper, as needed
- ½ of 1 Avocado, ripe
- ¼ cup Basil
- 2 tbsp. Chia Seeds
- 1 Garlic clove, minced

Directions:

⇒ To make this easy blended soup, place all the ingredients in a high-speed blender and blend for 3 minutes or until smooth.

⇒ Next, you can serve it cold, or you can warm it up on low heat for a few minutes.

Nutrition: [Calories: 250KcalProteins: 6.9gCarbohydrates: 18.4gFat: 18.1g]

31) Beets Gazpacho

Preparation Time: **Cooking Time:[10 Minutes]**   **Servings:[4]**

Ingredients:

- 1× 20oz. Can Great Northern Beans, rinsed and drained
- ¼ tsp. Kosher Salt
- 1 tbsp. Extra-Virgin Olive Oil
- ½ tsp. Garlic, fresh and minced
- 1× 6oz. pouch Pink Salmon flaked

- 2 tbsp. Lemon juice, freshly squeezed
- 4 Green Onions, sliced thinly
- ½ tsp. Ground Black Pepper
- ½ tsp. Lemon rind grated
- ¼ cup Flat-leaf Parsley, fresh and chopped

Directions:

⇒ First, place lemon rind, olive oil, lemon juice, black pepper, and garlic in a medium-sized mixing bowl and mix them with a whisker.

⇒ Combine beans, onions, salmon, and parsley in another medium-sized bowl and toss them well.

⇒ Then, spoon in the lemon juice dressing over the bean's mixture. Mix well `until the dressing coats the beans mixture.

⇒ Serve and enjoy.

Nutrition: [Calories 131KcalProteins:1.9gCarbohydrates: 14.8gFat: 8.5g]

32) Capellini Soup With Tofu And Shrimp

Preparation Time: **Cooking Time:[20 minutes]**   **Servings:[8]**

Ingredients:

- 4 cups of bok choy, sliced
- 1/4-pound shrimp, peeled, deveined
- 1 block firm tofu, sliced into squares
- 1 can sliced water chestnuts, drained
- 1 bunch scallions, sliced
- 2 cups reduced-sodium chicken broth

- 2 teaspoons soy sauce, reduced-sodium
- 2 cups capellini
- 2 teaspoons of sesame oil
- Freshly ground white pepper
- 1 teaspoon of rice wine vinegar

Directions:

⇒ Pour the broth in a saucepan over medium-high heat. Bring to a boil. Add the shrimp, bok choy, oil, and sauce. Allow to boil and turn the heat to low. Simmer for 5 minutes.

⇒ Add the water chestnuts, pepper, vinegar, tofu, capellini, and scallions. Cook for 5 minutes or until the capellini is barely tender. Serve while hot.

Nutrition: [Calories 205Carbs: 20gFat: 9gProtein: 9g]

33) Lemon Buttery Shrimp Rice

Preparation Time:	**Cooking Time:[10 Minutes]**	**Servings:[3]**

Ingredients:

- ¼ cup cooked wild rice
- ½ tsp. Butter divided
- ¼ tsp. olive oil
- 1 cup raw shrimps, shelled, deveined, drained

- ¼ cup frozen peas, thawed, rinsed, drained
- 1 Tbsp. lemon juice, freshly squeezed
- 1 Tbsp. chives, minced
- Pinch of sea salt, to taste

Directions:

⇒ Pour ¼ tsp. Butter and oil into wok set over medium heat. Add in shrimps and peas. Sauté until shrimps are coral pink, about 5 to 7 minutes.

⇒ Add in wild rice and cook until well heated—season with salt and butter.

⇒ Transfer to a plate. Sprinkle chives and lemon juice on top. Serve.

Nutrition: [Calories 510Carbs: 0gFat: 0gProtein: 0g]

34) Shrimp-lime Bake With Zucchini And Corn

Preparation Time:	**Cooking Time:[20 minutes]**	**Servings:[4]**

Ingredients:

- 1 tablespoon extra-virgin olive oil
- 2 small zucchinis, cut into ¼-inch dice
- 1 cup frozen corn kernels
- 2 scallions, thinly sliced
- 1 teaspoon salt

- ½ teaspoon ground cumin
- ½ teaspoon chipotle chili powder
- 1-pound peeled shrimp, thawed if necessary
- 1 tablespoon finely chopped fresh cilantro
- Zest and juice of 1 lime

Directions:

⇒ Preheat the oven to 400°F. Grease the baking sheet with the oil.

⇒ On the baking sheet, combine the zucchini, corn, scallions, salt, cumin, and chile powder and mix well. Arrange in a single layer.

⇒ Add the shrimp on top. Roast within 15 to 20 minutes.

⇒ Put the cilantro and lime zest and juice, stir to combine, and serve.

Nutrition: [Calories 184 Total Fat: 5g Total Carbohydrates: 11g Sugar: 3g Fiber: 2g Protein: 26g Sodium: 846mg]

35) Cauliflower Soup

Preparation Time:	**Cooking Time:[10 minutes]**	**Servings:[10]**

Ingredients:

- ¾ cup of water
- 2 teaspoon of olive oil
- 1 onion, diced
- 1 head of cauliflower, only the florets

- 1 can of full-fat coconut milk
- 1 teaspoon of turmeric
- 1 teaspoon of ginger
- 1 teaspoon raw honey

Directions:

⇒ Put all of the fixings into a large stockpot, and boil for about 10 minutes.

⇒ Use an immersion blender to blend and make the soup smooth. Serve.

Nutrition: [Total Carbohydrates 7g Dietary Fiber: 2g Net Carbs: Protein: 2g Total Fat: 11g Calories: 129]

36) Sweet Potato Black Bean Burgers

Preparation Time:	Cooking Time:[10 minutes]	Servings:[6]

Ingredients:

- 1/2 jalapeno, seeded and diced
- 1/2 cup quinoa
- 6 whole-grain hamburger buns
- 1 can black beans, rinsed and drained
- Olive oil/coconut oil, for cooking
- 1 sweet potato
- 1/2 cup red onion, diced
- 4 tablespoons gluten-free oat flour
- 2 cloves garlic, minced
- 2 teaspoons spicy cajun seasoning

- 1/2 cup cilantro, chopped
- 1 teaspoon cumin
- Sprouts
- Salt, to taste
- Pepper, to taste
- For the Crema:
- 2 tablespoons cilantro, chopped
- 1/2 ripe avocado, diced
- 4 tablespoons low-fat sour cream/plain Greek yogurt
- 1 teaspoon lime juice

Directions:

⇒ Rinse quinoa under cold running water. Put a cup of water in a saucepan and heat it. Add quinoa and bring to a boil.

⇒ Cover, then simmer over low heat until all of the water has absorbed, for about 15 minutes.

⇒ Turn the heat off and fluff quinoa with a fork. Then transfer quinoa to a bowl and let it cool for 5-10 minutes.

⇒ Poke potato with a fork and then microwave for a few minutes, until thoroughly cooked and soft. Once cooked, peel the potato and let it cool.

⇒ Add cooked potato to a food processor along with 1 can black beans, ½ cup chopped cilantro, 2 teaspoons of Cajun seasoning, ½ cup diced onion, 1 teaspoon cumin, and 2 minced cloves of garlic. Pulse until you obtain a smooth mixture. Transfer it to a bowl and add cooked quinoa.

⇒ Add in oat flour/oat bran. Mix well and shape into 6 patties. Put patties on a baking sheet and refrigerate for about half an hour.

⇒ Add all the Crema ingredients to a food processor. Pulse until smooth. Adjust salt to taste and refrigerate.

⇒ Grease a cooking pan with oil and heat it over medium heat. Cook each side of patties until light golden, just for 3-4 minutes. Serve with crema, sprouts, buns, and along with any of your favorite toppings.

Nutrition: [206 calories 6 g fat 33.9 g total carbs 7.9 g protein]

37) Coconut Mushroom Soup

Preparation Time:	Cooking Time:[10 minutes]	Servings:[3]

Ingredients:

- 1 tablespoon of coconut oil
- 1 tablespoon of ground ginger
- 1 cup of cremini mushrooms, chopped
- ½ teaspoon of turmeric

- 2 and ½ cups of water
- ½ cup of canned coconut milk
- Sea salt to taste

Directions:

⇒ Heat-up the coconut oil over medium heat in a large pot, and add the mushrooms. Cook for 3-4 minutes.

⇒ Put the remaining fixings and boil. Let it simmer for 5 minutes.

⇒ Divide between three soup bowls, and enjoy!

Nutrition: [Total Carbohydrates 4g Dietary Fiber: 1g Protein: 2g Total Fat: 14g Calories: 143]

38) Winter Style Fruit Salad

Preparation Time: **Cooking Time:[0 minutes]**   **Servings:[6]**

Ingredients:

- 4 cooked sweet potatoes, cubed (1-inch cubes)
- 3 pears, cubed (1-inch cubes)
- 1 cup of grapes, halved
- 1 apple, cubed
- ½ cup of pecan halves
- 2 tablespoons of olive oil
- 1 tablespoon of red wine vinegar
- 2 tablespoons of raw honey

Directions:

⇒ Mix the olive oil, red wine vinegar, then the raw honey to make the dressing, and set aside.

⇒ Combine the chopped fruit, sweet potato, and pecan halves, and divide this between six serving bowls.

⇒ Drizzle each bowl with the dressing.

Nutrition: [Total Carbohydrates 40g Dietary Fiber: 6g Protein: 3g Total Fat: 11g Calories: 251]

39) Honey-roasted Chicken Thighs With Carrots

Preparation Time: **Cooking Time:[50 Minutes]**   **Servings:[4]**

Ingredients:

- 2 tablespoons unsalted butter, at room temperature
- 3 large carrots, thinly sliced
- 2 garlic cloves, minced
- 4 bone-in, skin-on chicken thighs
- 1 teaspoon salt
- ½ teaspoon dried rosemary
- ¼ teaspoon freshly ground black pepper
- 2 tablespoons honey
- 1 cup chicken broth or vegetable broth
- Lemon wedges, for serving

Directions:

⇒ Preheat the oven to 400°F. Grease the baking sheet with the butter.

⇒ Arrange the carrots and garlic in a single layer on the baking sheet.

⇒ Put the chicken, skin-side up, on top of the vegetables, and season with the salt, rosemary, and pepper.

⇒ Put the honey on top and add the broth.

⇒ Roast within 40 to 45 minutes. Remove, then let it rest for 5 minutes, and serve with lemon wedges.

Nutrition: [Calories 428 Total Fat: 28g Total Carbohydrates: 15g Sugar: 11g Fiber: 2g Protein: 30g Sodium: 732mg]

40) Turkey Chili

Preparation Time: **Cooking Time: [4 Hours And 10 Minutes]**   **Servings:[8]**

Ingredients:

- 1-pound ground turkey, preferably 99% lean
- 2 cans of red kidney beans, rinsed & drained (15 oz each)
- 1 red pepper, chopped
- 2 cans of tomato sauce (15 oz each)
- 1 jar deli-sliced tamed jalapeno peppers, drained (16 oz)
- 2 cans of petite tomatoes, diced (15 oz each)
- 1 tablespoon cumin
- 1 yellow pepper, roughly chopped

- 2 cans of black beans, preferably rinsed & drained (15 oz each)
- 1 cup corn, frozen
- 2 tablespoon chili powder
- 1 tablespoon olive oil
- Black pepper & salt to taste
- 1 medium onion, diced
- Green onions, avocado, shredded cheese, Greek yogurt/sour cream, to top, optional

Directions:

⇒ Warm the oil until hot in a large skillet. Once done, carefully place the turkey into the hot skillet & cook until turn brown. Pour the turkey into the bottom of your slow cooker, preferably 6 quarts.

⇒ Add the jalapeños, corn, peppers, onion, diced tomatoes, tomato sauce, beans, cumin, and chili powder. Mix, then put pepper and salt to taste.

⇒ Cover & cook for 6 hours on low heat or 4 hours on high heat. Serve with the optional toppings and enjoy.

Nutrition: [kcal 455 Fat: 9 g Fiber: 19 g Protein: 38 g]

41) Lentil Soup With Spices

Preparation Time: **Cooking Time:[25 minutes]**   **Servings:[5]**

Ingredients:

- 1 Cup of yellow onion (cut into cubes)
- 1 Cup of carrot (cut into cubes)
- 1 Cup of turnip
- 2tbsp extra-virgin olive oil

- 2tbsp balsamic vinegar
- 4 cups of baby spinach
- 2 cups brown lentils
- ¼ Cup of fresh parsley

Directions:

⇒ Preheat the pressure cooker on medium flame and add olive oil and vegetables in it.

⇒ After 5 minutes, add broth, lentils, and salt in the pot and simmer for 15 minutes.

⇒ Remove the lid and add spinach and vinegar in it.

⇒ Stir the soup for 5 minutes and turn off the flame.

⇒ Garnish it with fresh parsley.

Nutrition: [Calories 96Carbs: 16gFat: 1gProtein: 4g]

42) Garlicky Chicken And Vegetables

Preparation Time: **Cooking Time:[45 Minutes]**   **Servings:[4]**

Ingredients:

- 2 teaspoons extra-virgin olive oil
- 1 leek, white part only, thinly sliced
- 2 large zucchinis, cut into ¼-inch slices
- 4 bone-in, skin-on chicken breasts
- 3 garlic cloves, minced

- 1 teaspoon salt
- 1 teaspoon dried oregano
- ¼ teaspoon freshly ground black pepper
- ½ cup white wine
- Juice of 1 lemon

Directions:

⇒ Preheat the oven to 400°F. Grease the baking sheet with the oil.

⇒ Place the leek and zucchini on the baking sheet.

⇒ Put the chicken, skin-side up, and sprinkle with the garlic, salt, oregano, and pepper. Add the wine.

⇒ Roast within 35 to 40 minutes. Remove and let rest for 5 minutes.

⇒ Add the lemon juice and serve.

Nutrition: [Calories 315 Total Fat: 8g Total Carbohydrates: 12g Sugar: 4g Fiber: 2g Protein: 44g Sodium: 685mg]

Fish & Seafood Recipes

43) White Fish Chowder With Vegetables

Preparation Time:	Cooking Time:[32 To 35 Minutes]	Servings:[6-8]

Ingredients:

- 3 sweet potatoes, peeled and cut into ½-inch pieces
- 4 carrots, peeled and cut into ½-inch pieces
- 3 cups full-fat coconut milk
- 2 cups water
- 1 teaspoon dried thyme
- ½ teaspoon sea salt
- 10½ ounces (298 g) white fish, skinless and firm, such as cod or halibut, cut into chunks

Directions:

⇒ Add the sweet potatoes, carrots, coconut milk, water, thyme, and sea salt to a large saucepan over high heat, and bring to a boil.

⇒ Reduce the heat to low, cover, and simmer for 20 minutes until the vegetables are tender, stirring occasionally.

⇒ Pour half of the soup to a blender and purée until thoroughly mixed and smooth, then return it to the pot.

⇒ Stir in the fish chunks and continue cooking for an additional 12 to 15 minutes, or until the fish is cooked through.

⇒ Remove from the heat and serve in bowls.

Nutrition: [calories: 450 ; fat: 28.7g ; protein: 14.2g ; carbs: 38.8g ; fiber: 8.1g ; sugar: 6.7g; sodium: 250mg]

44) Lemony Mussels

Preparation Time:	Cooking Time:	Servings:[4]

Ingredients:

- 1 tbsp. extra virgin extra virgin olive oil
- 2 minced garlic cloves
- 2 lbs. scrubbed mussels
- Juice of one lemon

Directions:

⇒ Put some water in a pot, add mussels, bring with a boil over medium heat, cook for 5 minutes, discard unopened mussels, and transfer them with a bowl.

⇒ In another bowl, mix the oil with garlic and freshly squeezed lemon juice, whisk well, and add over the mussels, toss and serve.

⇒ Enjoy!

Nutrition: [Calories: 140, Fat:4 g, Carbs:8 g, Protein:8 g, Sugars: 4g, Sodium:600 mg,]

45) Cheesy Tuna Pasta

Preparation Time:	Cooking Time:	Servings:[3-4]

Ingredients:

- 2 c. arugula
- ¼ c. chopped green onions
- 1 tbs. red vinegar
- 5 oz. drained canned tuna
- ¼ tsp. black pepper
- 2 oz. cooked whole-wheat pasta
- 1 tbsp. olive oil
- 1 tbsp. grated low-fat parmesan

Directions:

⇒ Cook the pasta in unsalted water until ready. Drain and set aside.

⇒ In a bowl of large size, thoroughly mix the tuna, green onions, vinegar, oil, arugula, pasta, and black pepper.

⇒ Toss well and top with the cheese.

⇒ Serve and enjoy.

Nutrition: [Calories: 566.3, Fat:42.4 g, Carbs:18.6 g, Protein:29.8 g, Sugars:0.4 g, Sodium:688.6 mg]

46) Trout With Cucumber Salsa

Preparation Time: **Cooking Time:[10 Minutes]**   **Servings:4**

Ingredients:

- Salsa:
- 1 English cucumber, diced
- ¼ cup unsweetened coconut yogurt
- 2 tablespoons chopped fresh mint
- 1 scallion, white and green parts, chopped
- 1 teaspoon raw honey
- Sea salt
- Fish:
- 4 (5-ounce) trout fillets, patted dry
- 1 tablespoon olive oil
- Sea salt and freshly ground black pepper, to taste

Directions:

⇒ Make the salsa: Stir together the yogurt, cucumber, mint, scallion, honey, and sea salt in a small bowl until completely mixed. Set aside.

⇒ On a clean work surface, rub the trout fillets lightly with sea salt and pepper.

⇒ Heat the olive oil in a large skillet over medium heat. Add the trout fillets to the hot skillet and panfry for about 10 minutes, flipping the fish halfway through, or until the fish is cooked to your liking.

⇒ Spread the salsa on top of the fish and serve.

Nutrition: [calories: 328 ; fat: 16.2g ; protein: 38.9g ; carbs: 6.1g ; fiber: 1.0g ; sugar: 3.2g; sodium: 477mg]

47) Lemon Zoodles With Shrimp

Preparation Time: **Cooking Time:[0 Minutes]**   **Servings:[4]**

Ingredients:

- Sauce:
- ½ cup packed fresh basil leaves
- Juice of 1 lemon (or 3 tablespoons)
- 1 teaspoon bottled minced garlic
- Pinch sea salt
- Pinch freshly ground black pepper
- ¼ cup canned full-fat coconut milk
- 1 large yellow squash, julienned or spiralized
- 1 large zucchini, julienned or spiralized
- 1 pound (454 g) shrimp, deveined, boiled, peeled, and chilled
- Zest of 1 lemon (optional)

Directions:

⇒ Make the sauce: Process the basil leaves, lemon juice, garlic, sea salt, and pepper in a food processor until chopped thoroughly.

⇒ Slowly pour in the coconut milk while the processor is still running. Pulse until smooth.

⇒ Transfer the sauce to a large bowl, along with the yellow squash and zucchini. Toss well.

⇒ Scatter the shrimp and lemon zest (if desired) on top of the noodles. Serve immediately.

Nutrition: [calories: 246 ; fat: 13.1g ; protein: 28.2g ; carbs: 4.9g ; fiber: 2.0g ; sugar: 2.8g; sodium: 139mg]

Meat Recipes

48) Pork With Nutmeg Squash

| Preparation Time: | Cooking Time:[35 Minutes] | Servings:[4] |

Ingredients:

- 1-pound pork stew meat, cubed
- 1 butternut squash, peeled and cubed
- 1 yellow onion, chopped
- 2 tablespoons olive oil
- 2 garlic cloves, minced
- ½ teaspoon garam masala
- ½ teaspoon nutmeg, ground
- 1 teaspoon chili flakes, crushed
- 1 tablespoon balsamic vinegar
- A pinch of sea salt and black pepper

Directions:

⇒ Heat up a pan with the oil over medium-high heat, add the onion and the garlic and sauté for 5 minutes.

⇒ Add the meat and brown for another 5 minutes.

⇒ Add the rest of the ingredients, toss, cook over medium heat for 25 minutes, divide between plates and serve.

Nutrition: [calories 348, fat 18.2, fiber 2.1, carbs 11.4, protein 34.3]

49) Creamy Pork And Tomatoes

| Preparation Time: | Cooking Time:[35 Minutes] | Servings:[4] |

Ingredients:

- 2 pounds pork stew meat, cubed
- 2 tablespoons avocado oil
- 1 cup tomatoes, cubed
- 1 cup coconut cream
- 1 tablespoon mint, chopped
- 1 jalapeno pepper, chopped
- A pinch of sea salt and black pepper
- 1 tablespoon hot pepper
- 2 tablespoons lemon juice

Directions:

⇒ Heat up a pan with the oil over medium heat, add the meat and brown for 5 minutes.

⇒ Add the rest of the ingredients, toss, cook over medium heat for 30 minutes more, divide between plates and serve.

Nutrition: [calories 230, fat 4, fiber 6, carbs 9, protein 14]

50) Lemon Tenderloin

| Preparation Time: | Cooking Time:[25 Minutes] | Servings:[2] |

Ingredients:

- ¼ teaspoon za'atar seasoning
- Zest of 1 lemon
- ½ teaspoon dried thyme
- ¼ teaspoon garlic powder
- ¼ teaspoon salt
- 1 tablespoon olive oil
- 1 (8-ounce / 227-g) pork tenderloin, sliver skin trimmed

Directions:

⇒ Preheat the oven to 425°F (220°C).

⇒ Combine the za'atar seasoning, lemon zest, thyme, garlic powder, and salt in a bowl, then rub the pork tenderloin with the mixture on both sides.

⇒ Warm the olive oil in an oven-safe skillet over medium-high heat until shimmering.

⇒ Add the pork tenderloin and sear for 6 minutes or until browned. Flip the pork halfway through the cooking time.

⇒ Arrange the skillet in the preheated oven and roast for 15 minutes or until an instant-read thermometer inserted in the thickest part of the tenderloin registers at least 145°F (63°C).

⇒ Transfer the cooked tenderloin to a large plate and allow to cool for a few minutes before serving.

Nutrition: [calories: 184 ; fat: 10.8g ; carbs: 1.2g ; fiber: 0g ; protein: 20.1g ; sodium: 358mg]

51) Chicken With Broccoli

Preparation Time: **Cooking Time:**   **Servings:[4]**

Ingredients:

- 1 chopped small white onion
- 1½ c. low-fat, low-sodium chicken broth
- Freshly ground black pepper

- 2 c. chopped broccoli
- 1 lb. cubed, skinless and de-boned chicken thighs
- 2 minced garlic cloves

Directions:

⇒ In a slow cooker, add all ingredients and mix well.

⇒ Set slow cooker on low.

⇒ Cover and cook for 4-5 hours.

⇒ Serve hot.

Nutrition: [Calories: 300, Fat:9 g, Carbs:19 g, Protein:31 g, Sugars:6 g, Sodium:200 mg]

52) Pork With Mushrooms And Cucumbers

Preparation Time: **Cooking Time:[25 Minutes]**   **Servings:[4]**

Ingredients:

- 2 tablespoons olive oil
- ½ teaspoon oregano, dried
- 4 pork chops
- 2 garlic cloves, minced
- Juice of 1 lime

- ¼ cup cilantro, chopped
- A pinch of sea salt and black pepper
- 1 cup white mushrooms, halved
- 2 tablespoons balsamic vinegar

Directions:

⇒ Heat up a pan with the oil over medium heat, add the pork chops and brown for 2 minutes on each side.

⇒ Add the rest of the ingredients, toss, cook over medium heat for 20 minutes, divide between plates and serve.

Nutrition: [calories 220, fat 6, fiber 8, carbs 14.2, protein 20]

53) Chicken Chopstick

Preparation Time: **Cooking Time:**   **Servings:[4]**

Ingredients:

- ¼ c. diced chopped onion
- 1 pack cooked chow Mein noodles
- Fresh ground pepper
- 2 cans cream mushroom soup

- 1 ¼ c. sliced celery
- 1 c. cashew nuts
- 2 c. cubed cooked chicken
- ½ c. water

Directions:

⇒ Preheat the oven to 375∘F.

⇒ In a pot suitable for the oven, pour in both cans of cream of mushroom soup and water. Mix until combined.

⇒ Add the cooked cubed chicken, onion, celery, pepper, cashew nuts to the soup. Stir until combined

⇒ Add half the noodles to the mixture, stir until coated.

⇒ Top the casserole with the rest of the noodles.

⇒ Place the pot in the oven. Bake for 25 minutes.

⇒ Serve immediately.

Nutrition: [Calories: 201, Fat:17 g, Carbs:15 g, Protein:13 g, Sugars:7 g, Sodium:10 mg]

54) Balsamic Roast Chicken

Preparation Time: **Cooking Time:**   **Servings:4**

Ingredients:

- 1 tbsp. minced fresh rosemary
- 1 minced garlic clove
- Black pepper
- 1 tbsp. olive oil

- 1 tsp. brown sugar
- 6 rosemary sprigs
- 1 whole chicken
- ½ c. balsamic vinegar

Directions:

⇒ Combine garlic, minced rosemary, black pepper and the olive oil. Rub the chicken with the herbal olive oil mixture.

⇒ Put 3 rosemary sprigs into the chicken cavity.

⇒ Place the chicken into a roasting pan and roast at 400F for about 1 hr. 30 minutes.

⇒ When the chicken is golden and the juices run clear, transfer to a serving dish.

⇒ In a saucepan dissolve the sugar in balsamic vinegar over heat. Do not boil.

⇒ Carve the chicken and top with vinegar mixture.

Nutrition: [Calories: 587, Fat:37.8 g, Carbs:2.5 g, Protein:54.1 g, Sugars:0 g, Sodium:600 mg]

55) Peach Chicken Treat

Preparation Time: **Cooking Time:**   **Servings:[4-5]**

Ingredients:

- 2 minced garlic cloves
- ¼ c. balsamic vinegar
- 4 sliced peaches
- 4 skinless, deboned chicken breasts

- ¼ c. chopped basil
- 1 tbsp. olive oil
- 1 chopped shallot
- ¼ tsp. black pepper

Directions:

⇒ Heat up the oil in a saucepan over medium-high flame.

⇒ Add the meat and season with black pepper; fry for 8 minutes on each side and set aside to rest in a plate.

⇒ In the same pan, add the shallot and garlic; stir and cook for 2 minutes.

⇒ Add the peaches; stir and cook for 4-5 more minutes.

⇒ Add the vinegar, cooked chicken, and basil; toss and simmer covered for 3-4 minutes more.

⇒ Serve warm.

Nutrition: [Calories: 270, Fat:0 g, Carbs:6.6 g, Protein:1.5 g, Sugars:24 g, Sodium:87 mg]

56) Ground Pork Pan

Preparation Time: **Cooking Time:[15 Minutes]**   **Servings:[4]**

Ingredients:

- 2 garlic cloves, minced
- 2 red chilies, chopped
- 2 tablespoons olive oil
- 2 pounds pork stew meat, ground
- 1 red bell pepper, chopped
- 1 green bell pepper, chopped

- 1 tomato, cubed
- ½ cup mushrooms, halved
- A pinch of sea salt and black pepper
- 1 tablespoon basil, chopped
- 2 tablespoons coconut aminos

Directions:

⇒ Heat up a pan with the oil over medium heat, add the garlic, chilies, bell peppers, tomato and the mushrooms and sauté for 5 minutes.

⇒ Add the meat and the rest of the ingredients, toss, cook over medium heat for 10 minutes more, divide between plates and serve.

Nutrition: [calories 200, fat 3, fiber 5, carbs 7, protein 17]

57) Parsley Pork And Artichokes

Preparation Time: **Cooking Time:[35 Minutes]**   **Servings:[4]**

Ingredients:

- 2 tablespoons balsamic vinegar
- 1 cup canned artichoke hearts, drained and quartered
- 2 tablespoons olive oil
- 2 pounds pork stew meat, cubed
- 2 tablespoons parsley, chopped

- 1 teaspoon cumin, ground
- 1 teaspoon turmeric powder
- 2 garlic cloves, minced
- A pinch of sea salt and black pepper

Directions:

⇒ Heat up a pan with the oil over medium heat, add the meat and brown for 5 minutes.

⇒ Add the artichokes, the vinegar and the other ingredients, toss, cook over medium heat for 30 minutes, divide between plates and serve.

Nutrition: [Calories 260, fat 5, fiber 4, carbs 11, protein 20]

58) Pork With Thyme Sweet Potatoes

Preparation Time: **Cooking Time:[35 Minutes]**   **Servings:[4]**

Ingredients:

- 2 sweet potatoes, peeled and cut into wedges
- 4 pork chops
- 3 spring onions, chopped
- 1 tablespoon thyme, chopped
- 2 tablespoons olive oil

- 4 garlic cloves, minced
- A pinch of sea salt and black pepper
- ½ cup vegetable stock
- ½ tablespoon chives, chopped

Directions:

⇒ In a roasting pan, combine the pork chops with the potatoes and the other ingredients, toss gently and cook at 390 degrees F for 35 minutes.

⇒ Divide everything between plates and serve.

Nutrition: [calories 210, fat 12.2, fiber 5.2, carbs 12, protein 10]

59) Curry Pork Mix

Preparation Time: **Cooking Time:[30 minutes]**   **Servings:[4]**

Ingredients:

- 2 tablespoon olive oil
- 4 scallions, chopped
- 2 garlic cloves, minced
- 2 pounds pork stew meat, cubed
- 2 tablespoons red curry paste

- 1 teaspoon chili paste
- 2 tablespoons balsamic vinegar
- ¼ cup vegetable stock
- ¼ cup parsley, chopped

Directions:

⇒ Heat up a pan with the oil over medium-high heat, add the scallions and the garlic and sauté for 5 minutes.

⇒ Add the remaining ingredients, toss, cook over medium heat for 20 minutes, divide between plates and serve.

⇒ Add the meat and brown for 5 minutes more.

Nutrition: [calories 220, fat 3, fiber 4, carbs 7, protein 12]

60) Stir-fried Chicken And Broccoli

Preparation Time: **Cooking Time:[10 minutes]**   **Servings:[4]**

Ingredients:

- 3 tablespoons extra-virgin olive oil
- 1½ cups broccoli florets
- 1½ pounds (680 g) boneless, skinless chicken breasts, cut into bite-size pieces
- ½ onion, chopped
- ½ teaspoon sea salt
- ⅛ teaspoon freshly ground black pepper
- 3 garlic cloves, minced
- 2 cups cooked brown rice

Directions:

⇒ Heat the olive oil in a large nonstick skillet over medium-high heat until shimmering.

⇒ Add the broccoli, chicken, and onion to the skillet and stir well. Season with sea salt and black pepper.

⇒ Stir-fry for about 8 minutes, or until the chicken is golden browned and cooked through.

⇒ Toss in the garlic and cook for 30 seconds, stirring constantly, or until the garlic is fragrant.

⇒ Remove from the heat to a plate and serve over the cooked brown rice.

Nutrition: [calories: 344 ; fat: 14.1g ; protein: 14.1g ; carbs: 40.9g ; fiber: 3.2g ; sugar: 1.2g ; sodium: 275mg]

61) Chicken And Broccoli

Preparation Time: **Cooking Time:**   **Servings:[4]**

Ingredients:

- 2 minced garlic cloves
- 4 de-boned, skinless chicken breasts
- ½ c. coconut cream
- 1 tbsp. chopped oregano
- 2 c. broccoli florets
- 1 tbsp. organic olive oil
- 1 c. chopped red onions

Directions:

⇒ Heat up a pan while using the oil over medium-high heat, add chicken breasts and cook for 5 minutes on each side.

⇒ Add onions and garlic, stir and cook for 5 minutes more.

⇒ Add oregano, broccoli and cream, toss everything, cook for ten minutes more, divide between plates and serve.

⇒ Enjoy!

Nutrition: [Calories: 287, Fat:10 g, Carbs:14 g, Protein:19 g, Sugars:10 g, Sodium:1106 mg]

62) Pork With Cabbage And Kale

Preparation Time: **Cooking Time:[35 Minutes]**   **Servings:[4]**

Ingredients:

- 1-pound pork stew meat, cut into strips
- 2 tablespoons olive oil
- 1 yellow onion, chopped
- A pinch of sea salt and black pepper
- cup green cabbage, shredded
- ½ cup baby kale
- 2 tablespoons oregano, dried
- 2 tablespoons balsamic vinegar
- ¼ cup vegetable stock

Directions:

⇒ Heat up a pan with the oil over medium-high heat, add the onion and the meat and brown for 5 minutes.

⇒ Add the cabbage and the other ingredients, toss gently and bake everything at 390 degrees F for 30 minutes.

⇒ Divide the whole mix between plates and serve.

Nutrition: [calories 331, fat 18.7, fiber 2.1, carbs 6.5, protein 34.2]

63) Mediterranean Chicken Bake With Vegetables

Preparation Time: **Cooking Time:[20 Minutes]**   **Servings:[4]**

Ingredients:

- 4 (4-ounce / 113-g) boneless, skinless chicken breasts
- 2 tablespoons avocado oil
- 1 cup sliced cremini mushrooms
- 1 cup packed chopped fresh spinach
- 1 pint cherry tomatoes, halved
- ½ cup chopped fresh basil
- ½ red onion, thinly sliced
- 4 garlic cloves, minced
- 2 teaspoons balsamic vinegar

Directions:

⇒ Preheat the oven to 400°F (205°C).

⇒ Arrange the chicken breast in a large baking dish and brush them generously with the avocado oil.

⇒ Mix together the mushrooms, spinach, tomatoes, basil, red onion, cloves, and vinegar in a medium bowl, and toss to combine. Scatter each chicken breast with ¼ of the vegetable mixture.

⇒ Bake in the preheated oven for about 20 minutes, or until the internal temperature reaches at least 165°F (74°C) and juices run clear when pierced with a fork.

⇒ Allow the chicken to rest for 5 to 10 minutes before slicing to serve.

Nutrition: [calories: 220 ; fat: 9.1g ; protein: 28.2g ; carbs: 6.9g ; fiber: 2.1g ; sugar: 6.7g ; sodium: 310mg]

64) Hidden Valley Chicken Drummies

Preparation Time: **Cooking Time:**   **Servings:[6-8]**

Ingredients:

- 2 tbsps. Hot sauce
- ½ c. melted butter
- Celery sticks
- 2 packages Hidden Valley dressing dry mix
- 3 tbsps. Vinegar
- 12 chicken drumsticks
- Paprika

Directions:

⇒ Preheat the oven to 350 0F.

⇒ Rinse and pat dry the chicken.

⇒ In a bowl blend the dry dressing, melted butter, vinegar and hot sauce. Stir until combined.

⇒ Place the drumsticks in a large plastic baggie, pour the sauce over drumsticks. Massage the sauce until the drumsticks are coated.

⇒ Place the chicken in a single layer on a baking dish. Sprinkle with paprika.

⇒ Bake for 30 minutes, flipping halfway.

⇒ Serve with crudité or salad.

Nutrition: [Calories: 155, Fat:18 g, Carbs:96 g, Protein:15 g, Sugars:0.7 g, Sodium:340 mg]

65) Balsamic Chicken And Beans

Preparation Time: **Cooking Time:**   **Servings:[4]**

Ingredients:

- 1 lb. trimmed fresh green beans
- ¼ c. balsamic vinegar
- 2 sliced shallots
- 2 tbsps. Red pepper flakes
- 4 skinless, de-boned chicken breasts
- 2 minced garlic cloves
- 3 tbsps. Extra virgin olive oil

Directions:

⇒ Combine 2 tablespoons of the olive oil with the balsamic vinegar, garlic, and shallots. Pour it over the chicken breasts and refrigerate overnight.

⇒ The next day, preheat the oven to 375 0F.

⇒ Take the chicken out of the marinade and arrange in a shallow baking pan. Discard the rest of the marinade.

⇒ Bake in the oven for 40 minutes.

⇒ While the chicken is cooking, bring a large pot of water to a boil.

⇒ Place the green beans in the water and allow them to cook for five minutes and then drain.

⇒ Heat one tablespoon of olive oil in the pot and return the green beans after rinsing them.

⇒ Toss with red pepper flakes.

Nutrition: [Calories: 433, Fat:17.4 g, Carbs:12.9 g, Protein:56.1 g, Sugars:13 g, Sodium:292 mg]

66) Italian Pork

Preparation Time: **Cooking Time:[1 Hour]**   **Servings:[6]**

Ingredients:

- 2 pounds pork roast
- 3 tablespoons olive oil
- 2 teaspoons oregano, dried
- 1 tablespoon Italian seasoning
- 1 teaspoon rosemary, dried

- 1 teaspoon basil, dried
- 3 garlic cloves, minced
- ¼ cup vegetable stock
- A pinch of salt and black pepper

Directions:

⇒ In a baking pan, combine the pork roast with the oil, the oregano and the other ingredients, toss and bake at 390 degrees F for 1 hour.

⇒ Slice the roast, divide it and the other ingredients between plates and serve.

Nutrition: [calories 580, fat 33.6, fiber 0.5, carbs 2.3, protein 64.9]

67) Chicken And Brussels Sprouts

Preparation Time: **Cooking Time:**   **Servings:[4]**

Ingredients:

- 1 cored, peeled and chopped apple
- 1 chopped yellow onion
- 1 tbsp. organic olive oil

- 3 c. shredded Brussels sprouts
- 1 lb. ground chicken meat
- Black pepper

Directions:

⇒ Heat up a pan while using oil over medium-high heat, add chicken, stir and brown for 5 minutes.

⇒ Add Brussels sprouts, onion, black pepper and apple, stir, cook for 10 minutes, divide into bowls and serve.

⇒ Enjoy!

Nutrition: [Calories: 200, Fat:8 g, Carbs:13 g, Protein:9 g, Sugars:3.3 g, Sodium:194 mg]

68) Chicken Divan

Preparation Time: **Cooking Time:**   **Servings:**

Ingredients:

- 1 c. croutons
- 1 c. cooked and diced broccoli pieces
- ½ c. water

- 1 c. grated extra sharp cheddar cheese
- ½ lb. de-boned and skinless cooked chicken pieces
- 1 can mushroom soup

Directions:

⇒ Preheat the oven to 350∘F

⇒ In a large pot, heat the soup and water. Add the chicken, broccoli, and cheese. Combine thoroughly.

⇒ Pour into a greased baking dish.

⇒ Place the croutons over the mixture.

⇒ Bake for 30 minutes or until the casserole is bubbling and the croutons are golden brown.

Nutrition: [Calories: 380, Fat:22 g, Carbs:10 g, Protein:25 g, Sugars:2 g, Sodium:475 mg]

69) Sumptuous Indian Chicken Curry

Preparation Time: **Cooking Time:[20 Minutes]** **Servings:[6]**

Ingredients:

- 2 tablespoons coconut oil, divided
- 2 (4-ounce / 113-g) boneless, skinless chicken breasts, cut into bite-size pieces
- 2 medium carrots, diced
- 1 small white onion, diced
- 1 tablespoon minced fresh ginger
- 6 garlic cloves, minced
- 1 cup sugar snap peas, diced
- 1 (5.4-ounce / 153-g) can unsweetened coconut cream

- 1 tablespoon sugar-free fish sauce
- 1 cup low-sodium chicken broth
- ½ cup diced tomatoes, with juice
- 1 tablespoon curry powder
- ¼ teaspoon sea salt
- Pinch cayenne pepper, to taste
- Freshly ground black pepper, to taste
- ¼ cup filtered water

Directions:

⇒ Heat 1 tablespoon of coconut oil in a nonstick skillet over medium-high heat until melted.

⇒ Add the chicken breasts to the skillet and cook for 15 minutes or until an instant-read thermometer inserted in the thickest part of the chicken breasts registers at least 165ºF (74ºC). Flip the chicken breasts halfway through the cooking time.

⇒ Meanwhile, in a separate skillet, heat the remaining coconut oil over medium heat until melted.

⇒ Add the carrots, onion, ginger, and garlic to the skillet and sauté for 5 minutes or until fragrant and the onion is translucent.

⇒ Add the peas, coconut cream, fish sauce, chicken broth, tomatoes, curry powder, salt, cayenne pepper, black pepper, and water to the skillet. Stir to mix well.

⇒ Bring to a boil. Reduce the heat to medium-low then simmer for 10 minutes.

⇒ Add the cooked chicken to the second skillet, then cook for 2 more minutes to combine well.

⇒ Pour the curry on a large serving plate, then serve immediately.

Nutrition: [calories: 223 ; fat: 15.7g ; protein: 13.4g ; carbs: 9.4g ; fiber: 3.0g ; sugar: 2.3g ; sodium: 673mg]

70) Pork With Balsamic Onion Sauce

Preparation Time: **Cooking Time:[35 Minutes]** **Servings:4**

Ingredients:

- 1 yellow onion, chopped
- 4 scallions, chopped
- 2 tablespoons avocado oil
- 1 tablespoon rosemary, chopped
- 1 tablespoon lemon zest, grated

- 2 pounds pork roast, sliced
- 2 tablespoons balsamic vinegar
- ½ cup vegetable stock
- A pinch of sea salt and black pepper

Directions:

⇒ Heat up a pan with the oil over medium heat, add the onion and the scallions and sauté for 5 minutes.

⇒ Add the rest of the ingredients except the meat, stir, and simmer for 5 minutes.

⇒ Add the meat, toss gently, cook over medium heat for 25 minutes, divide between plates and serve.

Nutrition: [calories 217, fat 11, fiber 1, carbs 6, protein 14]

71) Pork With Pears And Ginger

Preparation Time: **Cooking Time:[35 Minutes]**   **Servings:[4]**

Ingredients:

- 2 green onions, chopped
- 2 tablespoons avocado oil
- 2 pounds pork roast, sliced
- ½ cup coconut aminos

- 1 tablespoon ginger, minced
- 2 pears, cored and cut into wedges
- ¼ cup vegetable stock
- 1 tablespoon chives, chopped

Directions:

⇒ Heat up a pan with the oil over medium heat, add the onions and the meat and brown for 2 minutes on each side.

⇒ Add the rest of the ingredients, toss gently and bake at 390 degrees F for 30 minutes.

⇒ Divide the mix between plates and serve.

Nutrition: [calories 220, fat 13.3, fiber 2, carbs 16.5, protein 8]

72) Butter Chicken

Preparation Time: **Cooking Time:**   **Servings:[6]**

Ingredients:

- 8 finely chopped garlic cloves
- ¼ c. chopped low-fat unsalted butter
- Freshly ground black pepper

- 6 oz. skinless, de-boned chicken thighs
- 1 tsp. lemon pepper

Directions:

⇒ In a large slow cooker, place chicken thighs.

⇒ Top chicken thighs with butter evenly.

⇒ Sprinkle with garlic, lemon pepper and black pepper evenly.

⇒ Set the slow cooker on low.

⇒ Cover and cook for about 6 hours.

Nutrition: [Calories: 438, Fat:28 g, Carbs:14 g, Protein:30 g, Sugars:2 g, Sodium:700 mg]

73) Hot Chicken Wings

Preparation Time: **Cooking Time:**   **Servings:[4-5]**

Ingredients:

- 2 tbsps. Honey
- ½ stick margarine
- 2 tbsps. Cayenne pepper

- 1 bottle durkee hot sauce
- 10 - 20 chicken wings
- 10 shakes Tabasco sauce

Directions:

⇒ In a deep pot, heat the canola oil. Deep-fry the wings until cooked, approximately 20 minutes.

⇒ In a medium bowl, mix the hot sauce, honey, tabasco, and cayenne pepper. Mix well.

⇒ Place the cooked wings on paper towels. Drain the excess oil.

⇒ Toss the chicken wings in the sauce until coated evenly.

Nutrition: [Calories: 102, Fat:14 g, Carbs:55 g, Protein:23 g, Sugars:0.3 g, Sodium:340 mg]

74) Chicken, Pasta And Snow Peas

Preparation Time: **Cooking Time:**   **Servings:[1-2]**

Ingredients:

- Fresh ground pepper
- 2 ½ c. penne pasta
- 1 standard jar tomato and basil pasta sauce

- 1 c. halved and trimmed snow peas
- 1 lb. chicken breasts
- 1 tsp. olive oil

Directions:

⇒ In a medium frying pan, heat the olive oil. Season the chicken breasts with salt and pepper. Cook the chicken breasts until cooked through for approximately 5 – 7 minutes each side.

⇒ Cook the pasta according to instructions on package. Cook the snow peas with the pasta.

⇒ Scoop 1 cup of the pasta water. Drain the pasta and peas, set aside.

⇒ Once the chicken is cooked, slice diagonally.

⇒ Add the chicken back to the frying pan. Add the pasta sauce. If the mixture seems dry.

⇒ Add some of the pasta water to desired consistency. Heat together.

⇒ Divide into bowls and serve immediately.

Nutrition: [Calories: 140, Fat:17 g, Carbs:52 g, Protein:34 g, Sugars:2.3 g, Sodium:400 mg]

75) Apricot Chicken Wings

Preparation Time: **Cooking Time:**   **Servings:[3-4]**

Ingredients:

- 1 medium jar apricot preserve
- 1 package Lipton onion dry soup mix

- 1 medium bottle Russian dressing
- 2 lbs. chicken wings

Directions:

⇒ Pre-heat the oven to 350∘F.

⇒ Rinse and pat dry the chicken wings.

⇒ Place the chicken wings on a baking pan, single layer.

⇒ Bake for 45 – 60 minutes, turning halfway.

⇒ In a medium bowl, combine the Lipton soup mix, apricot preserve and Russian dressing.

⇒ Once the wings are cooked, toss with the sauce, until the pieces are coated.

⇒ Serve immediately with a side dish.

Nutrition: [Calories: 162, Fat:17 g, Carbs:76 g, Protein:13 g, Sugars:24 g, Sodium:700 mg]

76) Champion Chicken Pockets

Preparation Time: **Cooking Time:**   **Servings:[4]**

Ingredients:

- ½ c. chopped broccoli
- 2 halved whole wheat pita bread rounds
- ¼ c. bottled reduced-fat ranch salad dressing
- ¼ c. chopped pecans or walnuts

- 1 ½ c. chopped cooked chicken
- ¼ c. plain low-fat yogurt
- ¼ c. shredded carrot

Directions:

⇒ In a small bowl stir together yogurt and ranch salad dressing.

⇒ In a medium bowl combine chicken, broccoli, carrot, and, if desired, nuts. Pour yogurt mixture over chicken; toss to coat.

⇒ Spoon chicken mixture into pita halves.

Nutrition: [Calories: 384, Fat:11.4 g, Carbs:7.4 g, Protein:59.3 g, Sugars:1.3 g, Sodium:368.7 mg]

77) Stovetop Barbecued Chicken Bites

Preparation Time:	Cooking Time:	Servings:[4]

Ingredients:

- 1 diced medium bell pepper
- 1 tbsp. canola oil
- 1 c. tangy, spicy, and sweet barbecue sauce
- Freshly ground black pepper

- 1 diced medium onion
- 1 lb. de-boned skinless chicken breasts
- 3 minced garlic cloves

Directions:

⇒ Wash chicken breasts and pat dry. Cut into bite-sized chunks.

⇒ Heat oil in a large sauté pan over medium heat. Add chicken, onion, garlic, and bell pepper, and cook, stirring, for 5 minutes.

⇒ Add the barbecue sauce and stir to combine. Reduce heat to medium-low and cover pan. Cook, stirring frequently, until chicken is fully cooked, about 15 minutes.

⇒ Remove from heat. Season to taste with freshly ground black pepper and serve immediately.

Nutrition: [Calories: 191, Fat:5 g, Carbs:8 g, Protein:27 g, Sugars:0 g, Sodium:480 mg]

78) Chicken And Radish Mix

Preparation Time:	Cooking Time:	Servings:[4]

Ingredients:

- 10 halved radishes
- 1 tbsp. organic olive oil
- 2 tbsps. Chopped chives

- 1 c. low-sodium chicken stock
- 4 chicken things
- Black pepper

Directions:

⇒ Heat up a pan with all the oil over medium-high heat, add chicken, season with black pepper and brown for 6 minutes on either side.

⇒ Add stock and radishes, reduce heat to medium and simmer for twenty minutes.

⇒ Add the chives, toss, divide between plates and serve.

⇒ Enjoy!

Nutrition: [Calories: 247, Fat:10 g, Carbs:12 g, Protein:22 g, Sugars:1.1 g, Sodium:673 mg]

79) Chicken And Sweet Potato Stew

Preparation Time:	Cooking Time:[40 Minutes]	Servings:[4]

Ingredients:

- 1 tablespoon extra virgin olive oil
- 2 garlic cloves, sliced
- 1 white onion, chopped
- 14 ounces (397 g) tomatoes, chopped
- 2 tablespoons chopped rosemary leaves

- Sea salt and ground black pepper, to taste
- 4 free-range skinless chicken thighs
- 4 sweet potatoes, peeled and cubed
- 2 tablespoons basil leaves

Directions:

⇒ Preheat the oven to 375°F (190°C).

⇒ Heat the olive oil in a nonstick skillet over medium heat until shimmering.

⇒ Add the garlic and onion to the skillet and sauté for 5 minutes or until fragrant and the onion is translucent.

⇒ Add the tomatoes, rosemary, salt, and ground black pepper and cook for 15 minutes or until lightly thickened.

⇒ Arrange the chicken thighs and sweet potatoes on a baking sheet, then pour the mixture in the skillet over the chicken and sweet potatoes. Stir to coat well. Pour in enough water to make sure the liquid cover the chicken and sweet potatoes.

⇒ Bake in the preheated oven for 20 minutes or until the internal temperature of the chicken reaches at least 165°F (74°C).

⇒ Remove the baking sheet from the oven and pour them in a large bowl. Sprinkle with basil and serve.

Nutrition: [calories: 297 ; fat: 8.7g ; protein: 22.2g ; carbs: 33.1g ; fiber: 6.5g ; sugar: 9.3g; sodium: 532mg]

80) Rosemary Beef Ribs

Preparation Time: | **Cooking Time:[2 Hours]** | **Servings:[4]**

Ingredients:

- 1½ pounds (680 g) boneless beef short ribs
- ½ teaspoon garlic powder
- 1 teaspoon salt
- ½ teaspoon freshly ground black pepper
- 2 tablespoons olive oil
- 2 cups low-sodium beef broth
- 1 cup red wine
- 4 sprigs rosemary

Directions:

⇒ Preheat the oven to 350°F (180°C).

⇒ On a clean work surface, rub the short ribs with garlic powder, salt, and black pepper. Let stand for 10 minutes.

⇒ Heat the olive oil in an oven-safe skillet over medium-high heat.

⇒ Add the short ribs and sear for 5 minutes or until well browned. Flip the ribs halfway through. Transfer the ribs onto a plate and set aside.

⇒ Pour the beef broth and red wine into the skillet. Stir to combine well and bring to a boil. Turn down the heat to low and simmer for 10 minutes until the mixture reduces to two thirds.

⇒ Put the ribs back to the skillet. Add the rosemary sprigs. Put the skillet lid on, then braise in the preheated oven for 2 hours until the internal temperature of the ribs reads 165°F (74°C).

⇒ Transfer the ribs to a large plate. Discard the rosemary sprigs. Pour the cooking liquid over and serve warm.

Nutrition: [calories: 731 ; fat: 69.1g ; carbs: 2.1g ; fiber: 0g ; protein: 25.1g ; sodium: 781mg]

81) Chicken, Bell Pepper & Spinach Frittata

Preparation Time: | **Cooking Time:** | **Servings:[8]**

Ingredients:

- ¾ c. frozen chopped spinach
- ¼ tsp. garlic powder
- ¼ c. chopped red onion
- 1 1/3 c. finely chopped cooked chicken
- 8 eggs
- Freshly ground black pepper
- 1½ c. chopped and seeded red bell pepper

Directions:

⇒ Grease a large slow cooker.

⇒ In a bowl, add eggs, garlic powder and black pepper and beat well.

⇒ Place remaining ingredients into prepared slow cooker.

⇒ Pour egg mixture over chicken mixture and gently, stir to combine.

⇒ Cover and cook for about 2-3 hours.

Nutrition:

[Calories: 250.9, Fat:16.3 g, Carbs:10.8 g, Protein:16.2 g, Sugars:4 g, Sodium:486 mg]

Snack & Dessert Recipes

82) Dill And Salmon Pâté

Preparation Time: **Cooking Time:[0 Minutes]**   **Servings:[4]**

Ingredients:

- six ounces cooked salmon, bones and skin removed
- 1 Tablespoon chopped fresh dill
- ½ Teaspoon sea salt
- ¼ cup heavy (whipping) cream

Directions:

⇒ Take a blender or a food processor (or instead a large bowl using a mixer), mix the lemon zest, salmon, heavy cream, dill, and salt.

⇒ Blend till you attain the proper consistency for the smoothie.

Nutrition: [Carbohydrate 0.4gProtein; 25.8gTotal Fat: 12gCalories: 199Cholesterol: 0.0mgFiber: 0.8gSodium: 296mg]

83) Chai Spice Baked Apples

Preparation Time: **Cooking Time:[3 Hours]**   **Servings:[5]**

Ingredients:

- 5 apples
- ½ cup water
- ½ cup crushed pecans (optional)
- ¼ cup melted coconut oil
- 1 teaspoon ground cinnamon
- ½ teaspoon ground ginger
- ¼ teaspoon ground cardamom
- ¼ teaspoon ground cloves

Directions:

⇒ Core each apple, and peel off a thin strip from the top of each.

⇒ Add the water to the slow cooker. Gently place each apple upright along the bottom.

⇒ In a small bowl, stir together the pecans (if using), coconut oil, cinnamon, ginger, cardamom, and cloves.

⇒ Drizzle the mixture over the tops of the apples.

⇒ Cover the cooker and set to high. Cook for 2 to 3 hours, until the apples soften, and serve.

Nutrition: [Calories: 217Total Fat: 12gTotal Carbs: 30gSugar: 22g Fiber: 6g Protein: 0gSodium: 0mg]

84) Peach Dip

Preparation Time: **Cooking Time:[0 Minute]**   **Servings:[2]**

Ingredients:

- ½ cup nonfat: yogurt
- 1 cup peaches, chopped
- A pinch of cinnamon powder
- A pinch of nutmeg, ground

Directions:

⇒ In a bowl, combine the yogurt while using the peaches, cinnamon and nutmeg.

⇒ Whisk and divide into small bowls and serve.

Nutrition: [Calories: 165Fat: 2gFiber: 3gCarbs: 14gProtein: 13g]

85) Carrot And Pumpkin Seed Crackers

Preparation Time:	Cooking Time:[15 Minutes]	Servings:[40 Crackers]

Ingredients:

- 1⅓ cups pumpkin seeds
- ½ cup packed shredded carrot (about 1 carrot)
- 3 tablespoons chopped fresh dill
- ¼ teaspoon sea salt
- 2 tablespoons extra-virgin olive oil

Directions:

⇒ Preheat the oven to 350°F (180°C). Line a baking sheet with parchment paper.

⇒ Ground the pumpkin seeds in a food processor, then add the carrot, dill, salt, and olive oil to the food processor and pulse to combine well.

⇒ Pour them in the prepared baking sheet, then shape the mixture into a rectangle with a spatula.

⇒ Line a sheet of parchment paper over the rectangle, then flatten the rectangle to about ⅛ inch thick with a rolling pin.

⇒ Remove the parchment paper lined over the rectangle, then score it into 40 small rectangles with a sharp knife.

⇒ Arrange the baking sheet in the preheated oven and bake for 15 minutes or until golden browned and crispy.

⇒ Transfer the crackers on a large plate and allow to cool for a few minutes before serving.

Nutrition: [(4 crackers) calories: 130 ; fat: 11.9g ; protein: 5.1g ; carbs: 3.8g ; fiber: 1.0g ; sugar: 0g; sodium: 66mg]

86) Fresh Tomato, Onion And Jalapeno Pepper Salsa

Preparation Time:	Cooking Time:[0 Minute]	Servings:[4]

Ingredients:

- Cherry tomatoes, halved: 2 cups
- Red onion, peeled and chopped: ¼ cup
- Jalapeno pepper, chopped: 1
- Minced garlic: ½ teaspoon
- Chopped cilantro: 2 tablespoons
- Salt: ¼ teaspoon
- Ground black pepper: ¼ teaspoon
- Lime juice: 2 tablespoons

Directions:

⇒ Place all the ingredients for salsa in a medium bowl and stir until combined.

⇒ Serve straight away as a snack.

Nutrition: [Calories: 87Fat: 1gFiber: 2gCarbs: 7gProtein: 5g]

87) Easy Cranberry Compote

Preparation Time:	Cooking Time:[10 Minutes]	Servings:[4]

Ingredients:

- 4 cups fresh cranberries
- 1 tablespoon grated fresh ginger
- Juice of 2 oranges
- ¼ cup raw honey
- Zest of 1 orange

Directions:

⇒ Combine all the ingredients in a large pot. Stir to mix well.

⇒ Bring to a boil over medium-high heat, then cook for 10 more minutes or until it thickens and the cranberries pop.

⇒ Turn off the heat and allow to cool for a few minutes.

⇒ Pour them in a large bowl and serve warm.

Nutrition: [calories: 171 ; fat: 0.9g ; protein: 1.0g ; carbs: 38.8g ; fiber: 6.1g ; sugar: 29.5g ; sodium: 1mg]

88) Chickpeas And Pepper Hummus

Preparation Time: **Cooking Time:[0 minute]**   **Servings:[4]**

Ingredients:

- 14 ounces canned chickpeas, no-salt-added, drained and rinsed
- 1 tablespoon sesame paste
- 2 roasted red peppers, chopped
- Juice of ½ lemon
- 4 walnuts, chopped

Directions:

⇒ In your blender, combine the chickpeas with all the sesame paste, red peppers, lemon juice and walnuts, pulse well, divide into bowls and serve.

Nutrition: [Calories: 231Fat: 12gFiber: 6gCarbs: 15gProtein: 14g]

89) Protein Bars

Preparation Time: **Cooking Time:[0 minute]**   **Servings:[4]**

Ingredients:

- 4 ounces apricots, dried
- 2 ounces water
- 2 tablespoons rolled oats
- 1 tablespoon sunflower seeds
- 2 tablespoons coconut, shredded
- 1 tablespoon sesame seeds
- 1 tablespoon cranberries
- 3 tablespoons hemp seeds
- 1 tablespoon chia seeds

Directions:

⇒ In your food processor, combine the apricots while using water along with all the oats, pulse well, transfer for your bowl, add coconut, sunflower seeds, sesame seeds, cranberries, hemp and chia seeds and stir prior to getting a paste.

⇒ Roll this inside a log, wrap, cool inside fridge, slice and serve as a snack.

Nutrition: [Calories: 100Fat: 3gFiber: 4gCarbs: 8gProtein: 5g]

90) Sausage Vegetable Bake

Preparation Time: **Cooking Time:[20 minues]**   **Servings:[24]**

Ingredients:

- 1 cup mushrooms, quartered
- ¼ lb. smoked sausages, sliced
- 1 onion, sliced
- ¼ lb. Brussels sprouts
- 1 tbsp rosemary, chopped
- 1 tbsp thyme, chopped
- 2 garlic cloves, peeled only
- 1 tbsp olive oil
- Salt and black pepper to taste

Directions:

⇒ Prepare and set up the oven at 450 degrees F.

⇒ Toss all the veggies with the rest of the ingredients in a baking tray.

⇒ Bake for 20 minutes in the oven then stir in rosemary and thyme.

⇒ Serve.

Nutrition: [Calories 225 Fat 17.3g, Carbs 8.2g, Protein 7.3g, Fiber 1.3g]

91) Coconut Lemon Pudding

Preparation Time: **Cooking Time:[20 minutes]**   **Servings:[6]**

Ingredients:

- 3 cups coconut milk
- Juice of 2 lemons
- Lemon zest of 2 lemons
- ½ cup maple syrup
- 3 tablespoons coconut oil, melted
- 3 tablespoons flax meal mixed with 6 tablespoons water
- 4 drops lemon oil
- 2 tablespoons gelatin
- 1 cup water

Directions:

⇒ In your blender, mix coconut milk with lemon juice, lemon zest, maple syrup, coconut oil, flax meal, lemon oil and gelatin and pulse really well. Divide this into small jars and cover with lids then place them in a water bath and place in the oven

⇒ Cook at 350 degrees F for 20 minutes then cool and serve cold.

⇒ Enjoy!

Nutrition: [calories 171, fat 5, fiber 2, carbs 6, protein 8]

92) Blueberry Parfait

Preparation Time: **Cooking Time:[0 minute]**   **Servings:[4]**

Ingredients:

- 2 (14-ounce / 397-g) cans coconut cream, chilled
- 1 tablespoon pure maple syrup
- 1 tablespoon fresh lemon zest
- ½ teaspoon vanilla extract
- Sea salt, to taste
- For the Parfait:
- 2½ cups fresh blueberries

Directions:

⇒ Make the Cream

⇒ Whip the coconut cream in a large bowl with a hand mixer for 2 minutes or until the peaks form.

⇒ Then add the lemon zest, vanilla, maple syrup, and salt. Whip to combine well.

⇒ Make the Parfait

⇒ Pour half of the cream mixture in the bottom of a serving glass, then top with 1 cup of blueberries.

⇒ Spread the cream mixture on top of the blueberries, then top the cream with remaining blueberries.

⇒ Serve immediately.

Nutrition: [calories: 458 ; fat: 42.5g ; protein: 4.7g ; carbs: 22.6g ; fiber: 2.4g ; sugar: 12.4g ; sodium: 609mg]

93) Turmeric Gummies

Preparation Time: **Cooking Time:[10 minutes]**   **Servings:[6]**

Ingredients:

- 1 teaspoon ground turmeric
- 6 tablespoons maple syrup
- 8 tablespoons unflavored gelatin powder
- 3 ½ cups water

Directions:

⇒ In a pot, combine the water, turmeric, and maple syrup.

⇒ Bring to a boil for 5 minutes.

⇒ Remove from the heat and sprinkle with gelatin powder. Mix to hydrate the gelatin.

⇒ Turn on the heat and bring to a boil until the gelatin is completely dissolved.

⇒ Pour the mixture in a dish and chill the mixture in the fridge for at least 4 hours.

⇒ Once set, slice into small squares.

Nutrition: [Calories 68 Total Fat 0.03g Total Carbs 17g, Protein 0.2g Sugar 15g Fiber: 0.1g Sodium: 19mg Potassium 53mg]

94) Vegetable Mash With Basil

Preparation Time: **Cooking Time:[15 Minutes]**   **Servings:[24]**

Ingredients:

- ½ lb. celeriac, chopped
- 2 turnips, chopped
- 2 oz cream cheese
- 2 tbsp butter
- 1/3 cup sour cream
- ½ tsp garlic powder
- 1 tsp basil, chopped
- Salt and black pepper to taste

Directions:

⇒ Put a pot over medium-high heat and add turnips, celeriac, and enough water to cover them.

⇒ Cook the veggies to a boil then simmer for 15 minutes.

⇒ Drain the veggies and transfer to a bowl.

⇒ Mash the soft vegetables and stir in the rest of the ingredients.

⇒ Mix well and serve.

Nutrition: [Calories 223 Fat 13.5g, Carbs 12.3g, Protein 4g, Fiber 2.1g]

95) Spicy Kale Chips

Preparation Time: **Cooking Time:[20 minutes]**   **Servings:[4]**

Ingredients:

- 1 bunch curly kale, rinsed
- ¼ teaspoon ground cayenne pepper
- 1/8 teaspoon garlic powder
- spray oil for greasing
- ¼ teaspoon salt
- 1/8 teaspoon black pepper

Directions:

⇒ Preheat the oven to 3000F.

⇒ Pat dry the kale to remove water.

⇒ Tear the kale leaves into pieces, then place on a baking sheet lined with foil.

⇒ Spray with cooking oil and season with garlic powder, season, and black pepper.

⇒ Bake within 20 minutes. Serve.

Nutrition: [Calories 5 Total Fat 0.08g Total Carbs 1g Protein 0.4g Sugar 0.3g Fiber: 0.3g Sodium: 3mg Potassium 50mg]

96) Apple Muesli

Preparation Time: **Cooking Time:[0 minutes]**   **Servings:[4-6]**

Ingredients:

- 2 cups gluten-free rolled oats
- ¼ cup no-added-sugar apple juice
- 1¾ cups coconut milk
- 1 tablespoon apple cider vinegar
- 1 apple, cored and chopped
- Dash ground cinnamon

Directions:

⇒ Combine the oats, apple juice, coconut milk, and apple cider vinegar in a bowl. Stir to mix well. Wrap the bowl in plastic and refrigerate overnight.

⇒ Remove the bowl from the refrigerator. Top with apple and sprinkle with cinnamon, then serve.

Nutrition: [calories: 212 ; fat: 3.7g ; protein: 6.1g ; carbs: 38.9g ; fiber: 6.0g ; sugar: 10.0g ; sodium: 73mg]

97) Grape Cream

Preparation Time: **Cooking Time: 0 Minutes**   **Servings:[2]**

Ingredients:

- 1 pounds grapes
- ½ pound coconut cream
- A handful of fresh berries for serving

Directions:

⇒ In your food processor, puree the grapes with the cream and berries. Divide into small cups and serve.

⇒ Enjoy!

Nutrition: [calories 120, fat 9, fiber 3, carbs 10, protein 3]

98) Carrot Cake

Preparation Time: **Cooking Time:[0 Minutes]**   **Servings:[6]**

Ingredients:

- 1 cup pineapple, dried and chopped
- 2 carrots, chopped
- 1 ½ cups coconut flour
- 1 cup dates, pitted
- ½ cup shredded coconut, unsweetened
- ½ teaspoon ground cinnamon

Directions:

⇒ Put carrots in your food processor, pulse then add the flour, dates, pineapple, coconut and cinnamon.

⇒ Pulse again and spoon this into a cake pan, spread evenly and keep in the freezer for 3 hours before serving.

⇒ Enjoy!

Nutrition: [calories 160, fat 7, fiber 4, carbs 11, protein 4.]

99) Cashew Cake

Preparation Time: **Cooking Time:[0 minute]**   **Servings:[6]**

Ingredients:

- For the crust:
- ½ cup dates, pitted
- 1 tablespoon water
- ½ teaspoon vanilla extract
- ½ cup almonds
- For the cake:
- 3 cups cashews, soaked for 8 hours
- 1 cup blackberries
- ¾ cup maple syrup
- 1 tablespoon coconut oil, melted

Directions:

⇒ In your food processor, mix dates with water, vanilla and almonds and pulse well. Transfer the dough to a work surface and roll it out then transfer to a lined cake pan.

⇒ In your blender, mix the maple syrup with the coconut oil, cashews and berries. Blend well, spread evenly on the crust and place cake in the freezer for 5 hours, slice and serve.

⇒ Enjoy!

Nutrition: [calories 130, fat 5, fiber 5, carbs 12, protein 4]

100) Mini Spinach Muffins

Preparation Time: **Cooking Time:[15 Minutes]**   **Servings:[12 Muffins]**

Ingredients:

- 2 cups packed spinach
- ¼ cup raw honey
- 1 teaspoon vanilla extract
- 3 tablespoons extra-virgin olive oil
- 2 eggs
- 1 cup almond flour
- 1 cup oat flour
- 1 teaspoon baking soda
- 2 teaspoons baking powder
- ½ teaspoon salt
- Pinch freshly ground black pepper

Directions:

⇒ Preheat the oven to 350ºF (180ºC). Line a 12-cup muffin pan with paper muffin cups.

⇒ Put the spinach, honey, vanilla, and olive oil in a food processor, then break the eggs into it. Pulse to mix well until creamy and smooth.

⇒ Combine the flours, baking soda, baking powder, salt, and black pepper in a large bowl. Stir to mix well.

⇒ Make a well in the center of the flour mixture, then pour the spinach mixture into the well. Stir to mix well.

⇒ Divide the batter into muffin cups, then arrange the muffin pan in the preheated oven and bake for 15 minutes or until a toothpick inserted in the center comes out clean.

⇒ Remove the pan from the oven. Allow to cool for 10 minutes, then serve immediately.

Nutrition: [calories: 107 ; fat: 5.8g ; protein: 3.2g ; carbs: 11.9g ; fiber: 1.0g ; sugar: 5.5g ; sodium: 216mg]

101) Guacamole Stuffed Eggs

Preparation Time: **Cooking Time:[0 minute]**   **Servings:[4]**

Ingredients:

- 4 large eggs, boiled and peeled
- 4 bacon slices, cooked and crumbled
- 4 tbsp guacamole

- Salt to taste
- ¼ tsp chili powder
- 1 tbsp cilantro, chopped

Directions:

⇒ Cut the eggs in half and remove their yolk from inside.

⇒ Mash the yolks in a bowl and add bacon, guacamole, salt, cilantro and chili powder.

⇒ Mix well, then divide this yolk mixture into the egg whites.

⇒ Serve.

Nutrition: [Calories 223 Fat 17.9g, Carbs 1.2g, Protein 14.4g, Fiber 2.1g]

Special Recipes

102) Easy Sautéed Spinach

Preparation Time: **Cooking Time:[5 Minutes]**   **Servings:[4]**

Ingredients:

- 1 tablespoon extra-virgin olive oil
- 1 (10-ounce / 284-g) package frozen chopped spinach, thawed and drained
- 1 garlic clove, minced
- 1 teaspoon sea salt
- ¼ teaspoon freshly ground black pepper
- 1 tablespoon fresh lemon juice

Directions:

⇒ Heat the olive oil in a nonstick skillet over high heat until shimmering.

⇒ Add the spinach and garlic to the skillet, then sprinkle with salt and pepper. Sauté for 5 minutes or until the spinach is tender.

⇒ Transfer the sautéed spinach on a plate, then drizzle with lemon juice. Toss to combine well before serving.

Nutrition: [calories: 49 ; fat: 3.8g ; protein: 2.3g ; carbs: 3.0g ; fiber: 2.5g ; sugar: 0g; sodium: 631mg]

103) Zucchini Noodles

Preparation Time: **Cooking Time:[17 Minutes]**   **Servings:[4]**

Ingredients:

- 2 green zucchini
- 1 tablespoon olive oil
- 1 teaspoon water
- 1 tablespoon apple cider vinegar
- 1 teaspoon hot sauce
- 1 white onion
- 1 teaspoon salt
- ½ teaspoon turmeric
- ½ teaspoon thyme

Directions:

⇒ Wash the zucchini carefully and then make the noodles with a spiralizer.

⇒ Add the olive oil to a large pot.

⇒ Heat the oil well.

⇒ Transfer the zucchini noodles to a mixing bowl and sprinkle the mixture with the hot sauce, salt, turmeric, and thyme.

⇒ Stir the mixture carefully.

⇒ Peel the onion and slice it.

⇒ Toss the sliced onion into the preheated pan and cook over medium heat for 5 minutes. Stir it frequently.

⇒ Add the zucchini noodles.

⇒ Cook the mixture for 10 minutes more. Stir it frequently.

⇒ Combine the apple cider vinegar and water together. Stir the mixture.

⇒ Remove the zucchini mixture from the pan and transfer it to a serving bowl.

⇒ Sprinkle the dish with the apple cider vinegar mixture and stir it well.

⇒ Serve the zucchini noodles immediately.

Nutrition: [calories: 59, fat: 3.7g, total carbs: 6.2g, sugars: 2.9g, protein: 1.5g]

104) Leek With Sauce

Preparation Time: **Cooking Time:[12 minutes]** **Servings:[14]**

Ingredients:

- 3 tablespoon oyster sauce
- 1/3 teaspoon turmeric
- ¼ teaspoon ground white pepper
- 1-pound leek
- 1 teaspoon salt
- 1 tablespoon apple cider vinegar

- 1 cup water
- 1 teaspoon cilantro
- ½ teaspoon nutmeg
- 2 garlic cloves
- 1 teaspoon olive oil

Directions:

⇒ Wash the leek carefully and slice it.

⇒ Combine the sliced leek and nutmeg together in the mixing bowl.

⇒ Add the cilantro, apple cider vinegar, salt, ground white pepper, and turmeric.

⇒ Stir the mixture gently with your hands and leave it for 10 minutes to marinate.

⇒ Then preheat a skillet and add the olive oil.

⇒ Toss the sliced leek mixture in the skillet and fry it over high heat for 2 minutes.

⇒ Transfer the vegetables into a big pan and add the water.

⇒ Add the garlic cloves.

⇒ Simmer the dish for 10 minutes over medium heat.

⇒ Remove the dish from the heat and discard ½ of the liquid.

⇒ Add the oyster sauce and stir it well with a wooden spoon.

⇒ Serve the dish immediately.

Nutrition: [calories: 87, fat: 1.6g, total carbs: 17.4g, sugars: 4.8g, protein: 1.8g]

105) Roasted Rainbow Cauliflower

Preparation Time: **Cooking Time:[20 Minute]** **Servings:[4-6]**

Ingredients:

- 1½ cups white cauliflower florets
- 1½ cups yellow cauliflower florets
- 1½ cups purple cauliflower florets
- ¼ cup fresh lemon juice

- 3 tablespoons extra-virgin olive oil
- 1 teaspoon sea salt
- ¼ teaspoon freshly ground black pepper

Directions:

⇒ Preheat the oven to 400ºF (205ºC).

⇒ Add the cauliflower, lemon juice, and olive oil to a large bowl, and toss to combine.

⇒ Spread out the coated cauliflower on a rimmed baking sheet and season with salt and pepper.

⇒ Wrap in aluminum foil and bake in the preheated oven for 15 minutes. Remove the foil and bake for an additional 5 minutes, or until the tips and edges of the cauliflower are beginning to brown.

⇒ Let the cauliflower cool for 5 minutes before serving.

Nutrition: [calories: 121 ; fat: 10.5g ; protein: 2.5g ; carbs: 7.6g ; fiber: 2.1g ; sugar: 3.0g ; sodium: 621mg]

106) Loaded Cauliflower Soup

Preparation Time: **Cooking Time:[8 Hours]**   **Servings:[6]**

Ingredients:

- 1 cup celery, chopped
- 2 cups cauliflower, cut into florets
- 1 cup cucumber
- 3 cups chicken stocks
- 1 tbsp. garlic powder,
- 1 tbsp. bullion
- 1 tbsp. salt
- 1 tbsp. onion powder
- 1 tbsp. parsley flakes
- ½ cup heavy cream
- 1 ½ tbsp. butter
- 1 lb. bottom round steak

Directions:

⇒ Slice the celery into pieces then add them together with cauliflowers, cucumbers, and chicken in your slow cooker.

⇒ Add 3 tbsp. garlic, bullion, and 2 tbsp. seasoning salt, onion powder, and parsley flakes, then turn on high for 4-5 hours or low for 8-10 hours.

⇒ When halfway through with cooking, vegetables will be tender, so add heavy cream.

⇒ Using an immersion blender, puree your soup.

⇒ In a pan heat butter over medium-high heat, slice the steak into ½ inch cubes then season with garlic powder and salt.

⇒ Fry your steak in the pan with butter and add them in your slow cooker then continue cooking until ready.

⇒ Serve with bacon, sour cream, and shredded cheese as desired and enjoy.

Nutrition: [Calories 400Fat 26gCarbs 17gProtein 23gSugar 7gFiber 3gSodium 410mgPotassium 790mg]

107) Sweet Potatoes And Pea Hash

Preparation Time: **Cooking Time:[10 Minutes]**   **Servings:[4]**

Ingredients:

- 2 tablespoons coconut oil
- 3 garlic cloves, minced
- 4 scallions, sliced
- 2 teaspoons minced fresh ginger
- 1 teaspoon curry powder
- ½ teaspoon ground turmeric
- 1 teaspoon sea salt
- 2 medium sweet potatoes, roasted in their skins, peeled, and chopped
- 2 cups cooked brown rice
- 1 cup frozen peas
- 1 tablespoon coconut aminos
- ¼ cup chopped fresh cilantro, for garnish
- ½ cup chopped cashews, for garnish

Directions:

⇒ In a large skillet, melt the coconut oil over medium-high heat.

⇒ Add the garlic, scallions, ginger, curry powder, turmeric, and salt, and stir well. Sauté for 2 minutes until fragrant.

⇒ Fold in the sweet potatoes, brown rice, peas, and coconut aminos, and sauté for 5 minutes, stirring occasionally.

⇒ Sprinkle the cilantro and cashews on top for garnish and serve warm.

Nutrition: [calories: 510 ; fat: 17.1g ; protein: 11.2g ; carbs: 82.9g ; fiber: 10.0g ; sugar: 4.2g ; sodium: 634mg]

108) Almond Romesco Sauce

Preparation Time: **Cooking Time:[20 Minutes]**   **Servings:[2]**

Ingredients:

- 2 Red Bell Peppers, Chopped Rough
- 6 Cherry Tomatoes, Chopped Rough
- 3 Cloves Garlic, Chopped Rough
- ½ White Onion, Chopped Rough
- 1 Tablespoon Avocado Oil

- 1 cup Raw Almonds, Blanched
- ¼ Cup Olive Oil
- 2 Tablespoons Apple Cider Vinegar
- Sea Salt & Black Pepper to taste

Directions:

⇒ Turn your broiler to high and allow it to preheat. Get out a baking sheet and line it with foil.

⇒ Spread your tomatoes, onion, garlic, and bell pepper onto your baking sheet, and drizzle it with avocado oil. Broil this for ten minutes, and then get out a blender.

⇒ Pulse your almonds until they are crumbly.

⇒ Add in your olive oil, vinegar, vegetables, salt, and pepper. Process until smooth. It can keep in the fridge for up to five days. Alternatively, you can freeze it, and it will keep for three months.

Nutrition: [Calories 358Protein: 7.3 Grams Fat: 32.2 Grams Carbs: 13.7 Grams]

109) Radish Salad

Preparation Time: **Cooking Time:[0 minute]**   **Servings:[4]**

Ingredients:

- 2 cups radishes, sliced
- 2 spring onions, chopped
- A pinch of salt and black pepper
- 2 tablespoons balsamic vinegar

- 1 tablespoon chives, chopped
- 1 teaspoon rosemary, dried
- 2 tablespoons olive oil

Directions:

⇒ In a salad bowl, mix the radishes with the spring onions, salt, pepper and the other ingredients, toss and serve as a side salad.

Nutrition: [calories 110, fat 4, fiber 2, carbs 7, protein 7]

110) Crunchy Creamy Mashed Sweet Potatoes

Preparation Time: **Cooking Time:**   **Servings:[4]**

Ingredients:

- ¼ tsp. nutmeg
- 1 c. water
- 2 lbs. Sliced garnet sweet potatoes

- Sea flavored vinegar
- 2 tbsps. Maple syrup
- 3 tbsps. Vegan butter

Directions:

⇒ Peel the sweet potatoes and cut up into 1inch chunks

⇒ Pour 1 cup of water to the pot and add steamer basket

⇒ Add sweet potato chunks in the basket

⇒ Lock up the lid and cook on HIGH pressure for 8 minutes

⇒ Quick release the pressure

⇒ Open the lid and place the cooked sweet potatoes to the bowl

⇒ Use a masher to mash the potatoes

⇒ Add ¼ teaspoon of nutmeg, 2-3 tablespoons of unflavored vinegar butter, 2 tablespoon of maple syrup

⇒ Mash and mix

⇒ Season with flavored vinegar

⇒ Serve and enjoy!

Nutrition: [Calories: 249, Fat:8 g, Carbs:37 g, Protein:7 g, Sugars:13.9 g, Sodium:200 mg]

111) Egg And Bean Medley

Preparation Time: **Cooking Time:**   **Servings:[3]**

Ingredients:

- 5 beaten eggs
- 1 tsp. chili powder
- 2 chopped garlic cloves
- ½ c. milk
- ½ c. tomato sauce
- 1 c. cooked white beans

Directions:

⇒ Add milk and eggs to a bowl and mix well
⇒ Add the rest of the ingredients and mix well
⇒ Add a cup of water to the pot
⇒ Transfer the bowl to your pot and lock up the lid
⇒ Cook on HIGH pressure for 18 minutes
⇒ Release the pressure naturally over 10 minutes
⇒ Serve with warm bread
⇒ Enjoy!

Nutrition: [Calories: 206, Fat:9 g, Carbs:23 g, Protein:9 g, Sugars:0.6 g, Sodium:917.2 mg]

112) Satisfying Corn Cob

Preparation Time: **Cooking Time:**   **Servings:[8]**

Ingredients:

- 2 c. water
- 8 corn ears

Directions:

⇒ Husk the corns and cut the bottom part of the corns, wash them well thoroughly Wash well
⇒ Add water to the cooker base and arrange the corns vertically with the large part submerged underwater and the small part pointing upward
⇒ Lock up the lid and cook on HIGH pressure for 2 minutes
⇒ Release the pressure naturally
⇒ Serve with a bit of flavored vinegar and vegan butter

Nutrition: [Calories: 63, Fat:1 g, Carbs:14 g, Protein:2.4 g, Sugars:2.3 g, Sodium:2.5 mg]

113) Mediterranean Spice Rub

Preparation Time: **Cooking Time:[0 minute]**   **Servings:[¾ Cup]**

Ingredients:

- ¼ cup packed coconut sugar
- 3 tablespoons dried oregano leaves
- 2 tablespoons dried thyme leaves
- 1 tablespoon dried tarragon
- 1 teaspoon dried marjoram
- 1 teaspoon dried dill
- 1 teaspoon dried basil

Directions:

⇒ In a small bowl, stir together the coconut sugar, oregano, thyme, tarragon, marjoram, dill, and basil until well blended.
⇒ Store the seasoning in a sealed container for up to 1 month.

Nutrition: [(1 teaspoon)calories: 6 ; fat: 0g ; protein: 0g ; carbs: 1.1g ; fiber: 0g ; sugar: 0.8g ; sodium: 33mg]

114) Avocado Cilantro Detox Dressing

Preparation Time: **Cooking Time:[0 minute]**   **Servings:[3]**

Ingredients:

- 5 tablespoons lemon juice, freshly squeezed
- 1 clove of garlic, chopped
- 1 avocado, pitted and flesh scooped out
- 1 bunch cilantro, chopped
- ¼ teaspoon salt
- ¼ cup water

Directions:

⇒ Place all ingredients in a food processor and pulse until well combined.
⇒ Pulse until creamy.
⇒ Place in a lidded container and store in the fridge until ready to use.
⇒ Use on salads and sandwiches.

Nutrition: [Calories 114 Cal Fat: 10 g Carbs: 8 g Protein: 2 g Fiber: 5 g]

115) Mayonnaise

Preparation Time: **Cooking Time:[0 minute]** **Servings:1 cup**

Ingredients:

- 1 egg yolk
- 1 tablespoon apple cider vinegar
- ½ teaspoon Dijon mustard
- Pinch sea salt
- ¾ cup extra-virgin olive oil

Directions:

⇒ In a blender or food processor, combine the egg yolk, cider vinegar, mustard, and salt.

⇒ Turn on the blender or food processor and while it's running, remove the top spout.

⇒ Carefully, working one drip at a time to start, drip in the olive oil.

⇒ After about 15 drops, continue to run the processor and add the oil in a thin stream until emulsified.

⇒ You may adjust the amount of oil to adjust the thickness. The more oil you add, the thicker the mayonnaise will be.

⇒ Keep this refrigerated for up to 4 days in a tightly sealed container.

Nutrition: [Calories: 169Total Fat: 20gTotal Carbs: <1gSugar: 0g Fiber: 0g Protein: <1gSodium: 36mg]

Chapter 8: Anti-Inflammatory Meal Plan for Women

Day 1

1) Gluten free Crepes | Calories 100

19) Broccolini With Almonds | Calories 414

84) Peach Dip | Calories 165

48) Pork With Nutmeg Squash | Calories 348

103) Zucchini Noodles | Calories 59

Day 2

3) Savory Breakfast Pancakes | Calories 108

24) Bake Chicken Top-up with Olives, Tomatoes, And Basil | Calories 304

98) Carrot Cake | Calories 160

54) Balsamic Roast Chicken | Calories 587

110) Crunchy Creamy Mashed Sweet Potatoes | Calories 249

Day 3

7) Sweet Corn Muffins | Calories 203

33) Lemon Buttery Shrimp Rice | Calories 510

90) Sausage Vegetable Bake | Calories 225

60) Stir-fried Chicken And Broccoli | Calories 344

107) Sweet Potatoes And Pea Hash | Calories 510

Day 4

5) Chocolate Almond Flour And Peanut Butter Muffins | Calories 265

28) Cabbage Orange Salad With Citrusy Vinaigrette | Calories 70

82) Dill And Salmon Pâté | Calories 199

65) Balsamic Chicken And Beans | Calories 433

115) Mayonnaise | Calories 169

Day 5

13) Kale Turmeric Scramble | Calories 137

39) Honey-roasted Chicken Thighs With Carrots | Calories 428

93) Turmeric Gummies | Calories 68

77) Stovetop Barbecued Chicken Bites | Calories 191

102) Easy Sautéed Spinach | Calories 49

Day 6

10) Peaches with Honey Almond Kicotta | Calories 230

30) Green Soup | Calories 250

97) Grape Cream | Calories 120

71) Pork With Pears And Ginger | Calories 220

109) Radish Salad | Calories 110

Day 7

16) Carrot Cake Overnight Oats | Calories 340

41) Lentil Soup With Spices | Calories 96

100) Mini Spinach Muffins | Calories 107

80) Rosemary Beef Ribs | Calories 731

104) Leek With Sauce | Calories 87

Chapter 9: Conclusion

I hope this cookbook has allowed you to broaden your vision of all the possibilities you have at your fingertips to have a healthy life and leave behind the discomfort caused by inflammation.

I hope it is the first step in a new lifestyle that will allow you to enjoy your day-to-day life with more planning and significantly improve your quality of life, whether you are an office worker or an athlete, whether you live alone or with your family.

Remember that mealtime is a time to connect with yourself and become aware that what we eat and how we do it really says a lot about us and the way we take care of our body, the only one we will have for life.

If this cookbook has improved your life, remember to share it with your family, friends and colleagues, because sometimes a word is enough to change the lives of those around us for the better.

Keep in mind that if at this moment you do not give yourself the opportunity to start having a healthy diet, later will come the time of illness and negative consequences for your lack of care, so a healthy diet should not be a fad or something momentary but forever.

My most sincere good wishes, and may each recipe that you discovered here be a great experience of life and satisfy your palate.

Anti-Inflammatory Diet Cookbook For Men

A Body Sculpt Meal Plan On a Budget With Quick and Easy Recipes to Weight Loss and Prevent Prostate Cancer | Delicious Meal to Reduce Inflammation

By Annette Baker

Chapter 1: Introduction

There is a myth that men have no special dietary requirements, that they are more resilient and less prone to disease. The reality is that it is not so, men have special requirements in their diet, because of their metabolism, energy consumption and even hormonal changes. Precisely, the anti-inflammatory diet is perfect, because it provides the ideal nutritional contribution for men's needs.

This diet is beneficial for men because inflammation is the common root of numerous chronic pathological processes that men suffer in a higher percentage than women, such as cardiovascular diseases, cancer, Alzheimer's disease or joint inflammation with pain and functional limitation. It also prevents prostate cancer, which according to the American Cancer Society, by 2021 is projected 34,130 deaths due to prostate cancer, you can prevent it with this amazing diet.

What is an anti-inflammatory diet

An anti-inflammatory diet is a dietary regimen whose mission is focused on preventing and/or reducing inflammation in the body. It may be recommended as part of the treatment of a disease, such as an autoimmune disorder, prostate cancer, or simply be part of a healthy diet.

Which foods are allowed in the anti-inflammatory diet

The basis of the anti-inflammatory diet is a higher intake of vegetables, fruits, fish, legumes, poultry, tubers, seeds, whole grains, nuts and olive or coconut oil.

On the other hand, the foods that you should avoid or that are not allowed in the diet are: sodas, processed products, fried foods, sugar, refined flours, alcohol, refined carbohydrates, lard and partially hydrogenated fatty acids or trans fats.

How to start an anti-inflammatory diet
An anti-inflammatory diet is an ancestral diet that has been part of our diet for centuries, therefore it is in our genetic memory and is healthy for everyone. So, starting to follow it will be really easy, and in this cookbook you will find delicious recipes that will allow you to get started in a simple way.

Breakfast Recipes

1) Carrot Rice With Scrambled Eggs

Preparation Time: **Cooking Time: 3 Hours**   **Servings: 3**

Ingredients:

- For Sweet Tamari Soy Sauce
- 3 tbsp tamari sauce (gluten-free)
- 1 tbsp water
- 2-3 tbsp molasses
- For Spicy Mix-ins
- 3 garlic cloves
- 1 small shallot (sliced)
- 2 long red chilies
- Pinch of ground ginger
- For the Carrot Rice:
- 2 Tbsp sesame oil

- 5 eggs
- 4 large carrots
- 8 ounces sausage (chicken or any type of – gluten-free and minced).
- 1 tbsp sweet soy sauce
- 1 cup bean sprouts
- 1/2 cup fined diced broccoli
- salt and pepper to taste
- For Garnish:
- Cilantro
- Asian chili sauce
- Sesame seeds

Directions:

⇒ For the Sauce:

⇒ In a saucepan, boil molasses, water, and tamari at a high flame.

⇒ Lower the flame after the sauce boils and cook till molasses is completely dissolved.

⇒ Place the sauce in a separate bowl.

⇒ For the Carrot Rice:

⇒ In a bowl, combine ginger, garlic, onion, and red chilies.

⇒ To make rice out of the carrots, spiralize the carrots in a spiralizer.

⇒ Pulse the spiralized carrots in a food processor.

⇒ Cut broccoli into small dice like pieces

⇒ Add the sausage, carrots, broccoli, and the bean sprouts into the bowl of onion, ginger, garlic, and chilies.

⇒ Add the spicy mix of vegetables and the tamari sauce in the slow cooker pot.

⇒ Set the cooker on high heat for 3 hours or low heat for 6 hours.

⇒ Scramble two eggs in a non-stick frying pan or skillet.

⇒ Dish out the carrot rice and add scrambled eggs on top.

⇒ Garnish with sesame seeds, Asian chili sauce, and cilantro.

Nutrition: Calories 230 mg Total Fat: 13.7g Carbohydrates: 15.9g Protein: 12.2g Sugar: 8g Fiber 4.4g Sodium: 1060 mg Cholesterol: 239mg.

2) Egg Muffins With Feta And Quinoa

Preparation Time: **Cooking Time: 30 Minutes**   **Servings: 12**

Ingredients:

- Eggs, eight
- Tomatoes, chopped, one cup
- Salt, one quarter teaspoon
- Feta cheese, one cup
- Quinoa, one cup cooked

- Olive oil, two teaspoons
- Oregano, fresh chop, one tablespoon
- Black olives, chopped, one quarter cup
- Onion, chopped, one quarter cup
- Baby spinach, chopped, two cups

Directions:

⇒ Heat oven to 350. Spray oil a muffin pan with twelve cups. Cook spinach, oregano, olives, onion, and tomatoes for five minutes in the olive oil over medium heat. Beat eggs. Add the cooked mix of veggies to the eggs with the cheese and salt. Spoon mixture into muffin cups.

⇒ Bake thirty minutes. These will remain fresh in the fridge for two days. To eat, just wrap in a paper towel and warm in the microwave for thirty seconds.

Nutrition: Calorie 113 carbs 5 gramsprotein 6 gramsfat 7 gramssugar 1-gram

3) Delicious Turmeric Milk

Preparation Time: **Cooking Time: 5 Minutes**   **Servings: 2**

Ingredients:

- 1½ cups coconut milk, unsweetened
- 1½ cups almond milk, unsweetened
- ¼ teaspoon ground ginger
- 1½ teaspoon ground turmeric
- 1 tablespoon coconut oil
- ¼ teaspoon ground cinnamon

Directions:

⇒ Put the coconut and almond milk in a small pot and heat over medium heat, add the ginger, oil, turmeric and cinnamon.

⇒ Mix and cook for 5 minutes, divide into bowls and serve.

⇒ Enjoy!

Nutrition: calories 171, fat 3, fiber 4, carbs 6, protein 7

4) Green Shakshuka

Preparation Time: **Cooking Time: 25 Minutes**   **Servings: 4**

Ingredients:

- 2 tablespoons extra-virgin olive oil
- 1 onion, minced
- 2 garlic cloves, minced
- 1 jalapeño, seeded and minced
- 1-pound spinach (thawed if frozen)
- 1 teaspoon dried cumin
- ¾ teaspoon coriander
- Salt and freshly ground black pepper
- 2 tablespoons harissa
- ½ cup vegetable broth
- 8 large eggs
- Chopped fresh parsley, as needed for serving
- Chopped fresh cilantro, as needed for serving
- Red-pepper flakes, as needed for serving

Directions:

⇒ Preheat the oven to 350 ° F.

⇒ Heat the olive oil inside a large, oven-safe skillet, over medium heat. Add the onion and sauté for 4 to 5 minutes. Stir in the garlic and jalapeño, then sauté 1 minute more until fragrant.

⇒ Add the spinach and cook until fully wilted if fresh, 4 to 5 minutes or 1 to 2 minutes if thawed from frozen, until heated through.

⇒ Season with cumin, pepper, coriander, salt, and harissa. Cook for approximately 1 minute, until fragrant.

⇒ Switch the mixture to a food processor bowl or a blender and puree until it is coarse. Connect the broth and purée until smooth and thick.

⇒ Wipe the skillet out and dust it with nonstick cooking spray. Pour the spinach mixture into the pan back and make eight circular wells using a wooden spoon.

⇒ Crack the eggs in the pipes, softly. Switch the skillet to the oven and cook for 20 to 25 minutes until the egg whites are set fully, but the yolks are still a little jiggly.

⇒ Sprinkle with parsley, cilantro, and red pepper flakes on the shakshuka, to taste. Serve straight away.

Nutrition: 251 calories17g fat10g carbs17g protein3g sugars

5) Gingered Carrot & Coconut Muffins

Preparation Time: **Cooking Time: 20-22 Minutes**   **Servings:12**

Ingredients:

- 2 cups blanched almond flour
- ½ cup unsweetened coconut shreds
- 1 tsp baking soda
- ½ teaspoon allspice
- ½ teaspoon ground ginger
- Pinch of ground cloves
- Salt, to taste

- 3 organic eggs
- ½ cup organic honey
- ½ cup coconut oil
- 1 cup carrot, peeled and grated
- 2 tablespoons fresh ginger, peeled and grated
- ¾ cup raisins, soaked in water for 15 minutes and drained

Directions:

⇒ Preheat the oven to 350 degrees F. Grease 12 cups of a large muffin tin.

⇒ In a sizable bowl, mix together flour, coconut shreds, baking soda, spices and salt.

⇒ In another bowl, add eggs, honey, and oil and beat till well combined.

⇒ Add egg mixture into flour mixture and mix till well combined.

⇒ Fold in carrot, ginger and raisins.

⇒ Place the mix into prepared muffin cups evenly.

⇒ Bake approximately 20-22 minutes or till a toothpick inserted inside center arrives clean.

Nutrition: Calories: 352, Fat: 13g, Carbohydrates: 33g, Fiber: 9g, Protein: 15g

6) Hot Honey Porridge

Preparation Time: **Cooking Time:**   **Servings:4**

Ingredients:

- ¼ c. honey
- ½ c. rolled oats

- 3 c. boiling water
- ¾ c. bulgur wheat

Directions:

⇒ Place the bulgur wheat and rolled oats into a saucepan. Add the boiling water and stir to combine.

⇒ Place pan over high heat and bring to a boil. Once boiling, reduce heat to low, then cover and simmer for 10 minutes, stirring occasionally.

⇒ Remove from heat, stir in honey, and serve immediately.

Nutrition: Calories: 172, Fat:1 g, Carbs:40 g, Protein:4 g, Sugars:5 g, Sodium:20 mg

7) Breakfast Salad

Preparation Time: **Cooking Time: 0 Minutes**   **Servings:4**

Ingredients:

- 27 ounces kale salad mixed with dried fruit
- 1 ½ cups blueberries
- 15 ounces beets, cooked, peeled and cubed
- ¼ cup olive oil
- 2 tablespoons apple cider vinegar

- 1 teaspoon turmeric powder
- 1 tablespoon lemon juice
- 1 garlic clove, minced
- 1 teaspoon fresh grated ginger
- A pinch of black pepper

Directions:

⇒ In a salad bowl, mix the kale and dried fruit with beets and blueberries. In a separate bowl, mix the oil with the vinegar, turmeric, lemon juice, garlic, ginger and a pinch of black pepper, whisk well then pour over the salad, toss and serve.

⇒ Enjoy!

Nutrition: calories 188, fat 4, fiber 6, carbs 14, protein 7

8) Quick Quinoa With Cinnamon & Chia

Preparation Time: **Cooking Time: 3 Minutes**   **Servings:2**

Ingredients:

- 2-cups quinoa, pre-cooked
- 1-cup cashew milk
- ½-tsp ground cinnamon
- 1-cup fresh blueberries
- ¼-cup walnuts, toasted
- 2-tsp raw honey
- 1-Tbsp chia seeds

Directions:

⇒ Over medium-low heat, add the quinoa and cashew milk in a saucepan. Stir in the cinnamon, blueberries, and walnuts. Cook slowly for three minutes.

⇒ Remove the pan from the heat. Stir in the honey. Garnish with chia seeds on top before serving.

Nutrition: Calories 887Fat: 29.5gProtein: 44. Sodium: 85mgTotal Carbs: 129.3gDietary Fiber: 18.5g

9) Quinoa And Asparagus Mushroom Frittata

Preparation Time: **Cooking Time: 30 Minutes**   **Servings:3**

Ingredients:

- 2 tablespoons olive oil
- 1 cup sliced mushrooms
- 1 cup asparagus, cut into 1-inch pieces
- ½ cup chopped tomato
- 6 large eggs, pasture-raised
- 2 large egg whites, pasture-raised
- ¼ cup non-dairy milk
- 1 cup quinoa, cooked according to the package
- 3 tablespoons chopped basil
- 1 tablespoon chopped parsley, garnish
- Salt and pepper to taste

Directions:

⇒ Preheat the oven to 3500F.

⇒ In a skillet, heat the olive oil over medium flame.

⇒ Stir in the mushrooms and asparagus.

⇒ Season with salt and pepper to taste. Sauté for 7 minutes or until the mushrooms and asparagus have browned.

⇒ Add the tomatoes and cook for another 3 minutes. Set aside.

⇒ Meanwhile, mix the eggs, egg white, and milk in a mixing bowl. Set aside.

⇒ Place in a baking dish the quinoa and top with the vegetable mixture. Pour in the egg mixture.

⇒ Place in the oven and bake for 20 minutes or until the eggs have set.

Nutrition: Calories 450Total Fat 37gSaturated Fat 5gTotal Carbs 17gNet Carbs 14gProtein 12gSugar: 2gFiber: 3gSodium: 60mgPotassium 349mg

10) Spinach Mushroom Omelet

Preparation Time: **Cooking Time: 15 Minutes**   **Servings:2**

Ingredients:

- Olive oil, one tablespoon + one tablespoon
- Spinach, fresh, chopped, one- and one-half cup
- Green onion, one diced
- Eggs, three
- Feta cheese, one ounce
- Mushrooms, button, five sliced
- Red onion, diced, one quarter cup

Directions:

⇒ Sauté the mushrooms, onions, and spinach for three minutes in one tablespoon of olive oil and set to the side. Beat the eggs well and cook them in the other tablespoon of olive oil for three to four minutes until edges begin to brown.

⇒ Sprinkle all the other ingredients onto half of the omelet and fold the other half over the sautéed ingredients. Cook for one minute on each side.

Nutrition: Calories 337 fat 25 grams protein 22 grams carbs 5.4 grams sugar 1.3 grams fiber 1-gram

11) Pumpkin & Banana Waffles

Preparation Time: **Cooking Time: 5 Minutes**   **Servings:4**

Ingredients:

- ½ cup almond flour
- ½ cup coconut flour
- 1 tsp baking soda
- 1½ teaspoons ground cinnamon
- ¾ teaspoon ground ginger
- ½ teaspoon ground cloves
- ½ teaspoon ground nutmeg

- Salt, to taste
- 2 tablespoons olive oil
- 5 large organic eggs
- ¾ cup almond milk
- ½ cup pumpkin puree
- 2 medium bananas, peeled and sliced

Directions:

⇒ Preheat the waffle iron and after that grease it.

⇒ In a sizable bowl, mix together flours, baking soda and spices.

⇒ In a blender, add remaining ingredients and pulse till smooth.

⇒ Add flour mixture and pulse till

⇒ In preheated waffle iron, add required quantity of mixture.

⇒ Cook approximately 4-5 minutes.

⇒ Repeat using the remaining mixture.

Nutrition: Calories: 357.2, Fat: 28.5g, Carbohydrates: 19.7g, Fiber: 4g, Protein: 14g

12) Scrambled Eggs With Smoked Salmon

Preparation Time: **Cooking Time: 10 Minutes**   **Servings:2**

Ingredients:

- 4 eggs
- 2 tablespoons coconut milk
- Fresh chives, chopped

- 4 slices of wild-caught smoked salmon, chopped
- Salt to taste

Directions:

⇒ In a bowl, whisk the egg, coconut milk, and chives.

⇒ Grease the skillet with oil and heat over medium-low heat.

⇒ Pour the egg mixture and scramble the eggs while cooking.

⇒ When the eggs start to settle, add in the smoked salmon and cook for 2 more minutes.

Nutrition: Calories 349Total Fat 23gSaturated Fat 4gTotal Carbs 3gNet Carbs 1gProtein 29gSugar: 2gFiber: 2gSodium: 466mgPotassium 536mg

13) Creamy Parmesan Risotto With Mushroom And Cauliflower

Preparation Time: **Cooking Time: 18 Minutes**   **Servings:2**

Ingredients:

- 1 clove of garlic, peeled, sliced
- ½ cup heavy cream
- ½ cup cauliflower, riced

- ½ cup mushrooms, sliced
- Coconut oil, for frying
- Parmesan cheese, grated, for topping

Directions:

⇒ Take a skillet pan, place it over medium-high heat, add coconut oil and when it melts, add garlic and mushrooms and cook for 4 minutes or until sauté.

⇒ Then add cauliflower and cream into the pan, stir well and simmer for 12 minutes.

⇒ Transfer the risotto to a plate, top with cheese and then serve.

Nutrition: Calories 179, Total Fat 17.8g, Total Carbs 4.4g, Protein 2.8g, Sugar 2.1g, Sodium 61mg

14) Ranch Roasted Broccoli With Cheddar

Preparation Time: **Cooking Time: 30 Minutes**   **Servings:2**

Ingredients:

- 1½ cups broccoli florets
- Salt and freshly cracked black pepper, to taste
- 1/8 cup ranch dressing
- 1/8 cup heavy whipping cream
- ¼ cup shredded sharp cheddar cheese
- 1 tbsp olive oil

Directions:

⇒ Switch on the oven, then set its temperature to 375°F and let it preheat.

⇒ Meanwhile, take a medium bowl, add florets in it along with remaining ingredients and stir until well combined.

⇒ Take a casserole dish, grease it with oil, spoon in prepared mixture and bake for 30 minutes until thoroughly cooked.

⇒ When done, let casserole cool for 5 minutes and then serve.

Nutrition: Calories 111, Total Fat 7.7g, Total Carbs 5.7g, Protein 5.8g, Sugar 1.6g, Sodium 198mg

15) Power Protein Porridge

Preparation Time: **Cooking Time: 8 Minutes**   **Servings:2**

Ingredients:

- ¼-cup walnut or pecan halves, roughly chopped
- ¼-cup toasted coconut, unsweetened
- 2-Tbsps hemp seeds
- 2-Tbsps whole chia seeds
- ¾-cup almond milk, unsweetened
- ¼-cup coconut milk
- ¼-cup almond butter, roasted
- ½-tsp turmeric, ground
- 1-Tbsp extra virgin coconut oil or MCT oil
- 2-Tbsps erythritol or 5-10 drops liquid stevia (optional)
- A pinch of ground black pepper
- ½-tsp cinnamon or ½-tsp vanilla powder

Directions:

⇒ Put the walnuts, flaked coconut, and hemp seeds in a hot saucepan. Roast the mixture for 2 minutes, or until fragrant. Stir a few times to prevent burning. Transfer the roasted mix in a bowl. Set aside.

⇒ Combine the almond and coco milk in a small saucepan placed over medium heat. Heat the mixture.

⇒ After heating, but not boiling, switch off the heat. Add all the remaining ingredients. Mix well until thoroughly combined. Set aside for 10 minutes.

⇒ Combine half of the roasted mix with the porridge. Scoop the porridge into two serving bowls. Sprinkle each bowl with the remaining half of the roasted mixture and cinnamon powder. Serve the porridge immediately.

Nutrition: Calories 572Fat: 19gProtein: 28.6gSodium: 87mgTotal Carbs: 81.5gDietary Fiber: 10g

Lunch & Dinner Recipes

16)Smoked Salmon Salad

Preparation Time: **Cooking Time: 20 Minutes**   **Servings:4**

Ingredients:

- 2 baby fennel bulbs, thinly sliced, some fronds reserved
- 1 tablespoon salted baby capers, rinsed, drained
- ½ cup natural yogurt
- 2 tablespoons parsley, chopped
- 1 tablespoon lemon juice, freshly squeezed
- 2 tablespoons fresh chives, chopped
- 1 tablespoon chopped fresh tarragon
- 180g sliced smoked salmon, low-salt
- ½ red onion, sliced thinly
- 1 teaspoon lemon rind, finely grated
- ½ cup French green lentils, rinsed
- 60g fresh baby spinach
- ½ avocado, sliced
- A pinch of caster sugar

Directions:

⇒ Put water in a large saucepan with water and boil over moderate heat. Once boiling; cook the lentils until tender, for 20 minutes; drain well.

⇒ In the meantime, heat a chargrill pan over high heat in advance. Spray the fennel slices with some oil & cook until tender, for 2 minutes per side.

⇒ Process the chives, parsley, yogurt, tarragon, lemon rind, and capers in a food processor until completely smooth and then season with pepper to taste.

⇒ Place the onion with sugar, juice & a pinch of salt in a large-sized mixing bowl. Set aside for a couple of minutes and then drain.

⇒ Combine the lentils with onion, fennel, avocado, and spinach in a large-sized mixing bowl. Evenly divide among the plates and then top with the fish. Sprinkle with the leftover fennel fronds & more of fresh parsley. Drizzle with the green goddess dressing. Enjoy.

Nutrition: kcal 368 Fat: 14 g Fiber: 8 g Protein: 20 g

17)Bean Shawarma Salad

Preparation Time: **Cooking Time: 20 Minutes**   **Servings:2**

Ingredients:

- For Preparing Salad
- 20 Pita chips
- 5-ounces Spring lettuce
- 10 Cherry tomatoes
- ¾ Cup fresh parsley
- ¼ Cup red onion (chop)
- For Chickpeas
- 1tbsp Olive oil
- 1 Heading-tbsp cumin and turmeric
- ½ Heading-tbsp paprika and coriander powder
- 1 Pinch black pepper
- ½ Scant Kosher salt
- ¼tbsp Ginger and cinnamon powder
- For Preparing Dressing
- 3 Garlic Cloves
- 1tbsp Dried drill
- 1tbsp Lime juice
- Water
- ½ Cup hummus

Directions:

⇒ Place a rack in the already preheated oven (204C). Mix chickpeas with all spices and herbs.

⇒ Place a thin layer of chickpeas on the baking sheet and bake it almost for 20 minutes. Bake it until the beans are golden brown.

⇒ For preparing the dressing, mix all ingredients in a whisking bowl and blend it. Add water gradually for appropriate smoothness.

⇒ Mix all herbs and spices for preparing salad.

⇒ For serving, add pita chips and beans in the salad and drizzle some dressing over it.

Nutrition: Calories 173Carbs: 8gFat: 6gProtein: 19g

18) Pineapple Fried Rice

Preparation Time: **Cooking Time: 20 Minutes**   **Servings:4**

Ingredients:

- 2 carrots, peeled and grated
- 2 green onions, sliced
- 3 tablespoons soy sauce
- 1/2 cup ham, diced
- 1 tablespoon sesame oil
- 2 cups canned/fresh pineapple, diced
- 1/2 teaspoon ginger powder
- 3 cups brown rice, cooked
- 1/4 teaspoon white pepper
- 2 tablespoons olive oil
- 1/2 cup frozen peas
- 2 garlic cloves, minced
- 1/2 cup frozen corn
- 1 onion, diced

Directions:

⇒ Put 1 tablespoon sesame oil, 3 tablespoons soy sauce, 2 pinches of white pepper, and 1/2 teaspoon ginger powder in a bowl. Mix well and keep it aside.

⇒ Preheat oil in a skillet. Add the garlic along with the diced onion. Cook for about 3-4 minutes, stirring often.

⇒ Add 1/2 cup frozen peas, grated carrots, and 1/2 cup frozen corn. Stir until veggies are tender, just for few minutes.

⇒ Stir in soy sauce mixture, 2 cups of diced pineapple, ½ cup chopped ham, 3 cups cooked brown rice, and sliced green onions. Cook for about 2-3 minutes, stirring often. Serve!

Nutrition: 252 calories 12.8 g fat 33 g total carbs 3 g protein

19) Lentil Soup

Preparation Time: **Cooking Time: 30 Minutes**   **Servings:2**

Ingredients:

- 2 Carrots, medium & diced
- 2 tbsp. Lemon Juice, fresh
- 1 tbsp. Turmeric Powder
- 1/3 cup Lentils, cooked
- 1 tbsp. Almonds, chopped
- 1 Celery Stalk, diced
- 1 bunch of Parsley, chopped freshly
- 1 Yellow Onion, large & chopped
- Black Pepper, freshly grounded
- 1 Parsnip, medium & chopped
- ½ tsp. Cumin Powder
- 3 ½ cups Water
- ½ tsp. Pink Himalayan Salt
- 4 kale leaves, chopped roughly

Directions:

⇒ To start with, place carrots, parsnip, one tablespoon of water and onion in a medium-sized pot over medium heat.

⇒ Cook the vegetable mixture for 5 minutes while stirring it occasionally.

⇒ Next, stir in the lentils and spices into it. Combine well.

⇒ After that, pour water to the pot and bring the mixture to a boil.

⇒ Now, reduce the heat to low and allow it to simmer for 20 minutes.

⇒ Off the heat and remove it from the stove. Add the kale, lemon juice, parsley, and salt to it.

⇒ Then, give a good stir until everything comes together.

⇒ Top it with almonds and serve it hot.

Nutrition: Calories: 242KcalProteins: 10gCarbohydrates: 46gFat: 4g

20) Delicious Tuna Salad

Preparation Time: **Cooking Time: 15 Minutes**   **Servings:2**

Ingredients:

- 2 cans tuna packed in water (5oz each), drained
- ¼ cup mayonnaise
- 2 tablespoons fresh basil, chopped
- 1 tablespoon lemon juice, freshly squeezed
- 2 tablespoons fire-roasted red peppers, chopped
- ¼ cup kalamata or mixed olives, chopped
- 2 large vine-ripened tomatoes
- 1 tablespoon capers
- 2 tablespoons red onion, minced
- Pepper & salt to taste

Directions:

⇒ Add all the items (except tomatoes) together in a large-sized mixing bowl; give the ingredients a good stir until combined well. Slice the tomatoes into sixths and then gently pry it open.

⇒ Scoop the prepared tuna salad mixture into the middle; serve immediately & enjoy.

Nutrition: kcal 405 Fat: 24 g Fiber: 3.2 g Protein: 37 g

21) Aioli With Eggs

Preparation Time: **Cooking Time: 0 Minutes**   **Servings:12**

Ingredients:

- 2 egg yolks
- 1 garlic, grated
- 2 Tbsp. water
- ½ cup extra virgin olive oil
- ¼ cup lemon juice, fresh squeezed, pips removed
- ¼ tsp. sea salt
- Dash of cayenne pepper powder
- Pinch of white pepper, to taste

Directions:

⇒ Pour garlic, egg yolks, salt, and water into blender; process until smooth. Put in olive oil in a slow stream until dressing emulsifies.

⇒ Add in remaining ingredients. Taste; adjust seasoning if needed. Pour into an airtight container; use as needed.

Nutrition: Calories 100Carbs: 1gFat: 11gProtein: 0g

22) Brown Rice And Shitake Miso Soup With Scallions

Preparation Time: **Cooking Time: 45 Minutes**   **Servings:4**

Ingredients:

- 2 tablespoons sesame oil
- 1 cup thinly sliced shiitake mushroom caps
- 1 garlic clove, minced
- 1 (1½-inch) piece fresh ginger, peeled and sliced
- 1 cup medium-grain brown rice
- ½ teaspoon salt
- 1 tablespoon white miso
- 2 scallions, thinly sliced
- 2 tablespoons finely chopped fresh cilantro

Directions:

⇒ Heat-up the oil over medium-high heat in a large pot.

⇒ Add the mushrooms, garlic, and ginger and sauté until the mushrooms begin to soften about 5 minutes.

⇒ Put the rice and stir to coat with the oil evenly. Add 2 cups of water and salt and boil.

⇒ Simmer within 30 to 40 minutes. Use a little of the soup broth to soften the miso, then stir it into the pot until well blended.

⇒ Mix in the scallions plus cilantro, then serve.

Nutrition: Calories 265 Total Fat: 8g Total Carbohydrates: 43g Sugar: 2g Fiber: 3gProtein: 5gSodium: 456mg

23) Barbecued Ocean Trout With Garlic And Parsley Dressing

Preparation Time: **Cooking Time: 25 Minutes**   **Servings:8**

Ingredients:

- 3 ½ pounds piece of trout fillet, preferably ocean trout, boned, skin on
- 4 cloves of garlic, sliced thinly
- 2 tablespoons capers, coarsely chopped
- ½ cup flat-leaf parsley leaves, fresh
- 1 red chili, preferably long; sliced thinly
- 2 tablespoons lemon juice, freshly squeezed
- ½ cup olive oil
- Lemon wedges, to serve

Directions:

⇒ Brush the trout with approximately 2 tablespoons of oil; ensure that all sides are coated nicely. Preheat your barbecue over high heat, preferably with a closed hood. Decrease the heat to medium; place the coated trout on the barbecue plate, preferably on the skin-side. Cook until partially cooked and turn golden, for a couple of minutes. Carefully turn the trout; cook until cooked through, for 12 to 15 minutes, with the hood closed. Transfer the fillet to a large-sized serving platter.

⇒ In the meantime, heat the leftover oil; garlic over low heat in a small-sized saucepan until just heated through; garlic begins to change its color. Remove, then stir in the capers, lemon juice, chili. Drizzle the trout with the prepared dressing and then sprinkle with the fresh parsley leaves. Immediately serve with fresh lemon wedges, enjoy.

Nutrition: kcal 170 Fat: 30 g Fiber: 2 g Protein: 37 g

24) Buckwheat Noodle Soup

Preparation Time: **Cooking Time: 25 Minutes**   **Servings:4**

Ingredients:

- 2 cups Bok Choy, chopped
- 3 tbsp. Tamari
- 3 bundles of Buckwheat Noodles
- 2 cups Edamame Beans
- 7 oz. Shiitake Mushrooms, chopped
- 4 cups Water
- 1 tsp. Ginger, grated
- Dash of Salt
- 1 Garlic Clove, grated

Directions:

⇒ First, place water, ginger, soy sauce, and garlic in a medium-sized pot over medium heat.

⇒ Bring the ginger-soy sauce mixture to a boil and then stir in the edamame and shiitake to it.

⇒ Continue cooking for further 7 minutes or until tender.

⇒ Next, cook the soba noodles by following the Directions: given in the packet until cooked. Wash and drain well.

⇒ Now, add the bok choy to shiitake mixture and cook for further one minute or until the bok choy is wilted.

⇒ Finally, divide the soba noodles among the serving bowls and top it with the mushroom mixture.

Nutrition: Calories: 234KcalProteins: 14.2gCarbohydrates: 35.1gFat: 4g

25) Easy Salmon Salad

Preparation Time: **Cooking Time: 0 Minutes**   **Servings:1**

Ingredients:

- 1 cup of organic arugula
- 1 can of wild-caught salmon
- ½ of an avocado, sliced
- 1 tablespoon of olive oil
- 1 teaspoon of Dijon mustard
- 1 teaspoon of sea salt

Directions:

⇒ Start by whisking the olive oil, Dijon mustard, and sea salt together in a mixing bowl to make the dressing. Set aside.

⇒ Assemble the salad with the arugula as the base, and top with the salmon and sliced avocado.

⇒ Drizzle with the dressing.

Nutrition: Total Carbohydrates 7g Dietary Fiber: 5g Protein: 48g Total Fat: 37g Calories: 553

26) Vegetable Soup

Preparation Time: **Cooking Time: 40 Minutes**   **Servings:4**

Ingredients:

- 1 tbsp. Coconut Oil
- 2 cups Kale, chopped
- 2 Celery Stalks, diced
- ½ of 15 oz. can of White Beans, drained & rinsed
- 1 Onion, large & diced
- ¼ tsp. Black Pepper

- 1 Carrot, medium & diced
- 2 cups Cauliflower, cut into florets
- 1 tsp. Turmeric, grounded
- 1 tsp. Sea Salt
- 3 Garlic cloves, minced
- 6 cups Vegetable Broth

Directions:

⇒ To start with, heat oil in a large pot over medium-low heat.

⇒ Stir in the onion to the pot and sauté it for 5 minutes or until softened.

⇒ Put the carrot plus celery to the pot and continue cooking for another 4 minutes or until the veggies softened.

⇒ Now, spoon in the turmeric, garlic, and ginger to the mixture. Stir well.

⇒ Cook the veggie mixture for 1 minute or until fragrant.

⇒ Then, pour the vegetable broth along with salt and pepper and bring the mixture to a boil.

⇒ Once it starts boiling, add the cauliflower. Reduce the heat and simmer the vegetable mixture for 13 to 15 minutes or until the cauliflower is softened.

⇒ Finally, add the beans and kale—Cook within 2 minutes.

⇒ Serve it hot.

Nutrition: Calories 192KcalProteins:12.6gCarbohydrates: 24.6gFat: 6.4g

27) Lemony Garlic Shrimp

Preparation Time: **Cooking Time: 15 Minutes**   **Servings:4**

Ingredients:

- 1 and ¼ pounds shrimp, boiled or steamed
- 3 tablespoons garlic, minced
- ¼ cup lemon juice

- 2 tablespoons olive oil
- ¼ cup parsley

Directions:

⇒ Take a small skillet and place it over medium heat, add garlic and oil and stir cook for 1 minute.

⇒ Add parsley, lemon juice and season with salt and pepper accordingly.

⇒ Add shrimp in a large bowl and transfer the mixture from the skillet over the shrimp.

⇒ Chill and serve.

Nutrition: Calories: 130Fat: 3gCarbohydrates: 2gProtein: 22g

28) Brisket With Blue Cheese

Preparation Time: **Cooking Time: 8 Hrs. 10 Minutes**   **Servings:6**

Ingredients:

- 1 cup of water
- 1/2 tbsp garlic paste
- 1/4 cup soy sauce
- 1 ½ lb. corned beef brisket
- 1/3 teaspoon ground coriander

- 1/4 teaspoon cloves, ground
- 1 tbsp olive oil
- 1 shallot, chopped
- 2 oz. blue cheese, crumbled
- Cooking spray

Directions:

⇒ Place a pan over moderate heat and add oil to heat.

⇒ Toss in shallots and stir and cook for 5 minutes.

⇒ Stir in garlic paste and cook for 1 minute.

⇒ Transfer it to the slow cooker, greased with cooking spray.

⇒ Place brisket in the same pan and sear until golden from both sides.

⇒ Transfer the beef to the slow cooker along with other ingredients except for cheese.

⇒ Put on its lid and cook for 8 hrs. on low heat.

⇒ Garnish with cheese and serve.

Nutrition: Calories 397, Protein 23.5g, Fat 31.4g, Carbs 3.9g, Fiber 0 g

29) Baked Buffalo Cauliflower Chunks

Preparation Time: **Cooking Time: 35 Minutes**   **Servings:2**

Ingredients:

- ¼-cup water
- ¼-cup banana flour
- A pinch of salt and pepper
- 1-pc medium cauliflower, cut into bite-size pieces

- ½-cup hot sauce
- 2-Tbsp.s butter, melted
- Blue cheese or ranch dressing (optional)

Directions:

⇒ Preheat your oven to 425°F. Meanwhile, line a baking pan with foil.

⇒ Combine the water, flour, and a pinch of salt and pepper in a large mixing bowl.

⇒ Mix well until thoroughly combined.

⇒ Add the cauliflower; toss to coat thoroughly.

⇒ Transfer the mixture to the baking pan. Bake for 15 minutes, flipping once.

⇒ While baking, combine the hot sauce and butter in a small bowl.

⇒ Pour the sauce over the baked cauliflower.

⇒ Return the baked cauliflower to the oven, and bake further for 20 minutes.

⇒ Serve immediately with a ranch dressing on the side, if desired.

Nutrition: Calories: 168Cal Fat: 5.6gProtein: 8.4gCarbs: 23.8gFiber: 2.8g

30) Garlic Chicken Bake With Basil &tomatoes

Preparation Time: **Cooking Time: 30 Minutes**   **Servings:4**

Ingredients:

- ½ medium yellow onion
- 2tbsp Olive oil
- 3 Minced Garlic Cloves
- 1 Cup Basil (loosely cut)
- 1.lb Boneless chicken breast

- 14.5-ounces Italian chop tomatoes
- Salt & pepper
- 4 Medium zucchinis (spiralized into noodles)
- 1tbsp crushed red pepper
- 2tbsp Olive oil

Directions:

⇒ Pound the chicken pieces with a pan for fast cooking. Sprinkle salt, pepper, and oil on chicken pieces and marinate both sides of chicken equally.

⇒ Fry chicken pieces on a large hot skillet for 2-3 minutes on each side.

⇒ Sautee onion in the same skillet pan until it's brown. Add tomatoes, basil leaves, and garlic in it.

⇒ Simmer it for 3 minutes and add all spices and chicken in the skillet.

⇒ Serve it on the plate along with saucy zoodles.

Nutrition: Calories 44Carbs: 7gFat: 0gProtein: 2g

31) Creamy Turmeric Cauliflower Soup

Preparation Time: **Cooking Time: 15 Minutes**   **Servings: 4**

Ingredients:

- 2 tablespoons extra-virgin olive oil
- 1 leek, white part only, thinly sliced
- 3 cups cauliflower florets
- 1 garlic clove, peeled
- 1 (1¼-inch) piece fresh ginger, peeled and sliced
- 1½ teaspoons turmeric
- ½ teaspoon salt
- ¼ teaspoon freshly ground black pepper
- ¼ teaspoon ground cumin
- 3 cups vegetable broth
- 1 cup full-Fat: coconut milk
- ¼ cup finely chopped fresh cilantro

Directions:

⇒ Heat-up the oil over high heat in a large pot.

⇒ Sauté the leek within 3 to 4 minutes.

⇒ Put the cauliflower, garlic, ginger, turmeric, salt, pepper, and cumin and sauté for 1 to 2 minutes.

⇒ Put the broth, and boil.

⇒ Simmer within 5 minutes.

⇒ Purée the soup using an immersion blender until smooth.

⇒ Stir in the coconut milk and cilantro, heat through, and serve.

Nutrition: Calories 264 Total Fat: 23g Total Carbohydrates: 12g Sugar: 5g Fiber: 4gProtein: 7gSodium: 900mg

32) Mushroom, Kale, And Sweet Potato Brown Rice

Preparation Time: **Cooking Time: 50 Minutes**   **Servings: 4**

Ingredients:

- ¼ cup extra-virgin olive oil
- 4 cups coarsely chopped kale leaves
- 2 leeks, white parts only, thinly sliced
- 1 cup sliced mushrooms
- 2 garlic cloves, minced
- 2 cups peeled sweet potatoes cut into ½-inch dice
- 1 cup of brown rice
- 2 cups vegetable broth
- 1 teaspoon salt
- ¼ teaspoon freshly ground black pepper
- ¼ cup freshly squeezed lemon juice
- 2 tablespoons finely chopped fresh flat-leaf parsley

Directions:

⇒ Heat the oil over high heat.

⇒ Add the kale, leeks, mushrooms, and garlic and sauté until soft, about 5 minutes.

⇒ Add the sweet potatoes and rice and sauté for about 3 minutes.

⇒ Add the broth, salt, and pepper and boil. Simmer within 30 to 40 minutes.

⇒ Combine in the lemon juice and parsley, then serve.

Nutrition: Calories 425 Fat: 15g Total Carbohydrates: 65g Sugar: 6g Fiber: 6gProtein: 11gSodium: 1045mg

33) Baked Tilapia Recipe With Pecan Rosemary Topping

Preparation Time: **Cooking Time: 20 Minutes**   **Servings:4**

Ingredients:

- 4 tilapia fillets (4 ounces each)
- ½ teaspoon brown sugar or coconut palm sugar
- 2 teaspoons fresh rosemary, chopped
- 1/3 cup raw pecans, chopped
- A pinch of cayenne pepper
- 1 ½ teaspoon olive oil
- 1 large egg white
- 1/8 teaspoon salt
- 1/3 cup panko breadcrumbs, preferably whole-wheat

Directions:

⇒ Heat-up your oven to 350 F.

⇒ Stir the pecans with breadcrumbs, coconut palm sugar, rosemary, cayenne pepper, and salt in a small-sized baking dish. Add the olive oil; toss.

⇒ Bake within 7 to 8 minutes, until the mixture turns light golden brown.

⇒ Adjust the heat to 400 F and coat a large-sized glass baking dish with some cooking spray.

⇒ Whisk the egg white in the shallow dish. Work in batches; dip the fish (one tilapia at a time) into the egg white, and then, coating lightly into the pecan mixture. Put the coated fillets in the baking dish.

⇒ Press the leftover pecan mixture over the tilapia fillets.

⇒ Bake within 8 to 10 minutes. Serve immediately & enjoy.

Nutrition: Kcal 222 Fat: 10 g Fiber: 2 g Protein: 27 g

34) Black Bean Tortilla Wrap

Preparation Time: **Cooking Time: 0 Minutes**   **Servings:2**

Ingredients:

- ¼ cup of corn
- 1 handful of fresh basil
- ½ cup of arugula
- 1 tablespoon of nutritional yeast
- ¼ cup of canned black beans
- 1 peach, sliced
- 1 teaspoon of lime juice
- 2 gluten-free tortillas

Directions:

⇒ Divide the beans, corn, arugula, and peaches between the two tortillas.

⇒ Top each tortilla with half the fresh basil and lime juice

Nutrition: Total Carbohydrates 44g Dietary Fiber: 7g Protein: 8g Total Fat: 1g Calories: 203

35) White Bean Chicken With Winter Green Vegetables

Preparation Time: **Cooking Time: 45 Minutes**   **Servings:8**

Ingredients:

- 4 Garlic cloves
- 1tbsp Olive oil
- 3 medium parsnips
- 1kg Small cubes of chicken
- 1 Teaspoon cumin powder
- 2 Leaks & 1 Green part
- 2 Carrots (cut into cubes)
- 1 ¼ White kidney beans (overnight soaked)
- ½ Teaspoon dried oregano
- 2 Teaspoon Kosher salt
- Cilantro leaves
- 1 1/2tbsp Ground ancho chilies

Directions:

⇒ Cook garlic, leeks, chicken, and olive oil in a large pot on a medium flame for 5 minutes.

⇒ Now add carrots and parsnips, and after stirring for 2 minutes, add all seasoning ingredients.

⇒ Stir until the fragrant starts coming from it.

⇒ Now add beans and 5 cups of water in the pot.

⇒ Bring it to a boil and reduce the flame.

⇒ Allow it to simmer almost for 30 minutes and garnish with parsley and cilantro leaves.

Nutrition: Calories 263Carbs: 24gFat: 7g Protein: 26g

36) Herbed Baked Salmon

Preparation Time: **Cooking Time: 15 Minutes**   **Servings: 2**

Ingredients:

- 10 oz. Salmon Fillet
- 1 tsp. Olive Oil
- 1 tsp. Honey
- 1 tsp. Tarragon, fresh

- 1/8 tsp. Salt
- 2 tsp. Dijon Mustard
- ¼ tsp. Thyme, dried
- ¼ tsp. Oregano, dried

Directions:

⇒ Preheat the oven to 425 ° F.

⇒ After that, combine all the ingredients, excluding the salmon in a medium-sized bowl.

⇒ Now, spoon this mixture evenly over the salmon.

⇒ Then, place the salmon with the skin side down on the parchment paper-lined baking sheet.

⇒ Finally, bake for 8 minutes or until the fish flakes.

Nutrition: Calories: 239KcalProteins: 31gCarbohydrates: 3gFat: 11g

37) Valencia Salad

Preparation Time: **Cooking Time: 0 Minutes**   **Servings: 10**

Ingredients:

- 1 tsp. Kalamata olives in oil, pitted, drained lightly, halved, julienned
- 1 head, small Romaine lettuce, rinsed, spun-dried, sliced into bite-sized pieces
- ½ piece, small shallot, julienned
- 1 tsp. Dijon mustard
- ½ small satsuma or tangerine, pulp only

- 1 tsp. white wine vinegar
- 1 tsp. extra virgin olive oil
- 1 pinch fresh thyme, minced
- Pinch of sea salt
- Pinch of black pepper, to taste

Directions:

⇒ Combine vinegar, oil, fresh thyme, salt, mustard, black pepper, and honey, if using. Whisk well until dressing emulsifies a little.

⇒ Toss together the remaining salad ingredients in a salad bowl.

⇒ Drizzle dressing on top when about to serve. Serve immediately with 1 slice if sugar-free sourdough bread or saltine.

Nutrition: Calories 238Carbs: 23gFat: 15gProtein: 8g

38) "eat Your Greens" Soup

Preparation Time: **Cooking Time: 20 Minutes**   **Servings: 4**

Ingredients:

- ¼ cup extra-virgin olive oil
- 2 leeks, white parts only, thinly sliced
- 1 fennel bulb, trimmed and thinly sliced
- 1 garlic clove, peeled
- 1 bunch Swiss chard, coarsely chopped
- 4 cups coarsely chopped kale

- 4 cups coarsely chopped mustard greens
- 3 cups vegetable broth
- 2 tablespoons apple cider vinegar
- 1 teaspoon salt
- ¼ teaspoon freshly ground black pepper
- ¼ cup chopped cashews (optional)

Directions:

⇒ Heat-up the oil over high heat in a large pot.

⇒ Add the leeks, fennel, and garlic and sauté until softened, for about 5 minutes.

⇒ Add the Swiss chard, kale, and mustard greens and sauté until the greens wilt, 2 to 3 minutes.

⇒ Put the broth and boil.

⇒ Simmer within 5 minutes.

⇒ Stir in the vinegar, salt, pepper, and cashews (if using).

⇒ Purée the soup using an immersion blender until smooth and serve.

Nutrition: Calories 238 Total Fat: 14g Total Carbohydrates: 22g Sugar: 4g Fiber: 6gProtein: 9gSodium: 1294mg

39) Miso Salmon And Green Beans

Preparation Time: **Cooking Time: 25 Minutes**   **Servings:4**

Ingredients:

- 1 tablespoon sesame oil
- 1-pound green beans, trimmed
- 1-pound skin-on salmon fillets, cut into 4 steaks
- ¼ cup white miso
- 2 teaspoons gluten-free tamari or soy sauce
- 2 scallions, thinly sliced

Directions:

⇒ Preheat the oven to 400°F. Grease the baking sheet with the oil.

⇒ Put the green beans, then the salmon on top of the green beans, and brush each piece with the miso.

⇒ Roast within 20 to 25 minutes.

⇒ Drizzle with the tamari, sprinkle with the scallions, and serve.

Nutrition: Calories 213 Total Fat: 7g Total Carbohydrates: 13g Sugar: 3g Fiber: 5g Protein: 27g Sodium: 989mg

40) Leek, Chicken, And Spinach Soup

Preparation Time: **Cooking Time: 15 Minutes**   **Servings:4**

Ingredients:

- 3 tablespoons unsalted butter
- 2 leeks, white parts only, thinly sliced
- 4 cups baby spinach
- 4 cups chicken broth
- 1 teaspoon salt
- ¼ teaspoon freshly ground black pepper
- 2 cups shredded rotisserie chicken
- 1 tablespoon thinly sliced fresh chives
- 2 teaspoons grated or minced lemon zest

Directions:

⇒ Dissolve the butter over high heat in a large pot.

⇒ Add the leeks and sauté until softened and beginning to brown, 3 to 5 minutes.

⇒ Add the spinach, broth, salt, and pepper and boil.

⇒ Simmer within 1 to 2 minutes.

⇒ Put the chicken and cook within 1 to 2 minutes.

⇒ Sprinkle with the chives and lemon zest and serve.

Nutrition: Calories 256 Total Fat: 12g Total Carbohydrates: 9g Sugar: 3g Fiber: 2gProtein: 27gSodium: 1483mg

41) Dark Choco Bombs

Preparation Time: **Cooking Time: 5 Minutes**   **Servings:24**

Ingredients:

- 1 cup heavy cream
- 1 cup cream cheese softened
- 1 teaspoon vanilla essence
- 1/2 cup dark chocolate
- 2 oz. Stevia

Directions:

⇒ Melt chocolate in a bowl by heating in a microwave.

⇒ Beat the rest of the ingredients in a mixer until fluffy, then stir in the chocolate melt.

⇒ Mix well, then divide the mixture in a muffin tray lined with muffin cups.

⇒ Refrigerate for 3 hrs.

⇒ Serve.

Nutrition: Calories 97 Fat 5 g, Carbs 1 g, Protein 1 g, Fiber 0 g

42) Italian Stuffed Peppers

Preparation Time: **Cooking Time: 40 Minutes**   **Servings:6**

Ingredients:

- 1 teaspoon garlic powder
- 1/2 cup mozzarella, shredded
- 1 lb. lean ground meat
- 1/2 cup parmesan cheese
- 3 bell peppers, cut into half lengthwise, stems, seeds and ribs removed

- 1 (10 oz.) package frozen spinach
- 2 cups marinara sauce
- 1/2 teaspoon salt
- 1 teaspoon Italian seasoning

Directions:

⇒ Coat a foil-lined baking sheet with non-stick spray. Place the peppers on the baking pan.

⇒ Add turkey to a non-stick pan and cook over medium heat until no longer pink.

⇒ When almost cooked, add 2 cups of marinara sauce and seasonings—Cook for about 8-10 minutes.

⇒ Add spinach along with 1/2 cup parmesan cheese. Stir until well-combined.

⇒ Add half cup of the meat mixture into each pepper and divide cheese among all—Preheat the oven to 450 F.

⇒ Bake peppers for about 25-30 minutes. Cool, and serve.

Nutrition: 150 calories 2 g fat 11 g total carbs 20 g protein

43) Smoked Trout Wrapped In Lettuce

Preparation Time: **Cooking Time: 45 Minutes**   **Servings:4**

Ingredients:

- ¼ Cup salt-roasted potatoes
- 1 cup grape tomatoes
- ½ Cup basil leaves
- 16 small & medium size lettuce leaves
- 1/3 cup Asian sweet chili
- 2 Carrots

- 1/3 Cup Shallots (thin sliced)
- ¼ Cup thin slice Jalapenos
- 1tbsp Sugar
- 2-4.5 Ounces skinless smoked trout
- 2tbsp Fresh lime Juice
- 1 Cucumber

Directions:

⇒ Cut carrots and cucumber in slim strip size.

⇒ Marinate these vegetables for 20 mins with sugar, fish sauce, lime juice, shallots, and jalapeno.

⇒ Add trout pieces and other herbs in this vegetable mixture and blend.

⇒ Strain water from vegetable and trout mixture and again toss it to blend.

⇒ Place lettuce leaves on a plate and transfer trout salad on them.

⇒ Garnish this salad with peanuts and chili sauce.

Nutrition: Calories 180Carbs: 0gFat: 12gProtein: 18g

Fish & Seafood Recipes

44) Broiled Sea Bass

Preparation Time: **Cooking Time:**   **Servings:2**

Ingredients:

- 2 minced garlic cloves
- Pepper.
- 1 tbsp. lemon juice

- 2 white sea bass fillets
- ¼ tsp. herb seasoning blend

Directions:

⇒ Spray a broiler pan with some olive oil and place the fillets on it.

⇒ Sprinkle the lemon juice, garlic and the spices over the fillets.

⇒ Broil for about 10 min or until the fish is golden.

⇒ Serve over a bed of sautéed spinach if desired.

Nutrition: Calories: 169, Fat:9.3 g, Carbs:0.34 g, Protein:15.3 g, Sugars:0.2 g, Sodium:323 mg

45) Spicy Cod

Preparation Time: **Cooking Time:**   **Servings:4**

Ingredients:

- 2 tbsps. Fresh chopped parsley
- 2 lbs. cod fillets

- 2 c. low sodium salsa
- 1 tbsp. flavorless oil

Directions:

⇒ Preheat the oven to 350°F.

⇒ In a large, deep baking dish drizzle the oil along the bottom. Place the cod fillets in the dish. Pour the salsa over the fish. Cover with foil for 20 minutes. Remove the foil last 10 minutes of cooking.

⇒ Bake in the oven for 20 – 30 minutes, until the fish is flaky.

⇒ Serve with white or brown rice. Garnish with parsley.

Nutrition: Calories: 110, Fat:11 g, Carbs:83 g, Protein:16.5 g, Sugars:0 g, Sodium:122 mg

46) Smoked Trout Spread

Preparation Time: **Cooking Time:**   **Servings:2**

Ingredients:

- 2 tsps. Fresh lemon juice
- ½ c. low-fat cottage cheese
- 1 diced celery stalk
- ¼ lb. skinned smoked trout fillet,

- ½ tsp. Worcestershire sauce
- 1 tsp. hot pepper sauce
- ¼ c. coarsely chopped red onion

Directions:

⇒ Combine the trout, cottage cheese, red onion, lemon juice, hot pepper sauce and Worcestershire sauce in a blender or food processor.

⇒ Process until smooth, stopping to scrape down the sides of the bowl as needed.

⇒ Fold in the diced celery.

⇒ Keep in an air-tight container in the refrigerator.

Nutrition: Calories: 57, Fat:4 g, Carbs:1 g, Protein:4 g, Sugars:0 g, Sodium:660 mg

47) Tuna And Shallots

Preparation Time: **Cooking Time:**   Servings:4

Ingredients:

- ½ c. low-sodium chicken stock
- 1 tbsp. olive oil
- 4 boneless and skinless tuna fillets
- 2 chopped shallots
- 1 tsp. sweet paprika
- 2 tbsps. lime juice
- ¼ tsp. black pepper

Directions:

⇒ Heat up a pan with the oil over medium-high heat, add shallots and sauté for 3 minutes.

⇒ Add the fish and cook it for 4 minutes on each side.

⇒ Add the rest of the ingredients, cook everything for 3 minutes more, divide between plates and serve.

Nutrition: Calories: 4040, Fat:34.6 g, Carbs:3 g, Protein:21.4 g, Sugars:0.5 g, Sodium:1000 mg

48) Hot Tuna Steak

Preparation Time: **Cooking Time:**   Servings:6

Ingredients:

- 2 tbsps. Fresh lemon juice
- Pepper.
- Roasted orange garlic mayonnaise
- ¼ c. whole black peppercorns
- 6 sliced tuna steaks
- 2 tbsps. Extra-virgin olive oil
- Salt

Directions:

⇒ Place the tuna in a bowl to fit. Add the oil, lemon juice, salt and pepper. Turn the tuna to coat well in the marinade. Let rest 15 to 20 minutes, turning once.

⇒ Place the peppercorns in a double thickness of plastic bags. Tap the peppercorns with a heavy saucepan or small mallet to crush them coarsely. Place on a large plate.

⇒ When ready to cook the tuna, dip the edges into the crushed peppercorns. Heat a nonstick skillet over medium heat. Sear the tuna steaks, in batches if necessary, for 4 minutes per side for medium-rare fish, adding 2 to 3 tablespoons of the marinade to the skillet if necessary, to prevent sticking.

⇒ Serve dolloped with roasted orange garlic mayonnaise

Nutrition: Calories: 124, Fat:0.4 g, Carbs:0.6 g, Protein:28 g, Sugars:0 g, Sodium:77 mg

Meat Recipes

49) Roast Chicken Dal

Preparation Time: **Cooking Time:**   **Servings:4**

Ingredients:

- 15 oz. rinsed lentils
- ¼ c. low-fat plain yogurt
- 1 minced small onion
- 4 c. de-boned, skinless and roasted chicken

- 2 tsps. Curry powder
- 1 ½ tsps. Canola oil
- 14 oz. fire-roasted diced tomatoes
- ¼ tsp. salt

Directions:

⇒ Heat oil in a large heavy saucepan over medium-high heat.

⇒ Add onion and cook, stirring, until softened but not browned, 3 to 4 minutes.

⇒ Add curry powder and cook, stirring, until combined with the onion and intensely aromatic, 20 to 30 seconds.

⇒ Stir in lentils, tomatoes, chicken and salt and cook, stirring often, until heated through.

⇒ Remove from the heat and stir in yogurt. Serve immediately.

Nutrition: Calories: 307, Fat:6 g, Carbs:30 g, Protein:35 g, Sugars:0.1 g, Sodium:361 mg

50) Oregano Pork

Preparation Time: **Cooking Time: 8 Hours**   **Servings:4**

Ingredients:

- 2 pounds pork roast, sliced
- 2 tablespoons oregano, chopped
- ¼ cup balsamic vinegar
- 1 cup tomato paste
- 1 tablespoon sweet paprika

- 1 teaspoon onion powder
- 2 tablespoons chili powder
- 2 garlic cloves, minced
- A pinch of salt and black pepper

Directions:

⇒ In your slow cooker, combine the roast with the oregano, the vinegar and the other ingredients, toss, put the lid on and cook on Low for 8 hours.

⇒ Divide everything between plates and serve.

Nutrition: calories 300, fat 5, fiber 2, carbs 12, protein 24

51) Chicken And Avocado Bake

Preparation Time: **Cooking Time:**   **Servings:4**

Ingredients:

- 2 thinly sliced green onion stalks
- Mashed avocado
- 170 g non-fat Greek yogurt

- 1 ¼ g salt
- 4 chicken breasts
- 15 g blackened seasoning

Directions:

⇒ Start by putting your chicken breast in a plastic zip lock bag with the blackened seasoning. Close and shake, then marinate for about 2-5 minutes.

⇒ As your chicken is marinating, go ahead and put your Greek Yogurt, mashed avocado, and salt in your blender and pulse until smooth.

⇒ Place a large skillet or cast-iron pan on the stove at medium heat, oil the pan and cook the chicken until it is cooked through. You'll need about 5 minutes on each side. However, try not to dry the juices and plate it as soon as the meat is cooked.

⇒ Top with the yogurt mixture.

Nutrition: Calories: 296, Fat:13.5 g, Carbs:6.6 g, Protein:35.37 g, Sugars:0.8 g, Sodium:173 mg

52) Five-spice Roasted Duck Breasts

Preparation Time: **Cooking Time:**   **Servings:4**

Ingredients:

- 1 tsp. five-spice powder
- ¼ tsp. cornstarch
- 2 orange juice and zest
- 1 tbsp. reduced-sodium soy sauce

- 2 lbs. de-boned duck breast
- ½ tsp. kosher salt
- 2 tsps. Honey

Directions:

⇒ Preheat oven to 375 0F.

⇒ Place duck skin-side down on a cutting board. Trim off all excess skin that hangs over the sides. Turnover and make three parallel, diagonal cuts in the skin of each breast, cutting through the fat but not into the meat. Sprinkle both sides with five-spice powder and salt.

⇒ Place the duck skin-side down in an ovenproof skillet over medium-low heat.

⇒ Cook until the fat is melted and the skin is golden brown, about 10 minutes. Transfer the duck to a plate; pour off all the fat from the pan. Return the duck to the pan skin-side up and transfer to the oven.

⇒ Roast the duck for 10 to 15 minutes for medium, depending on the size of the breast, until a thermometer inserted into the thickest part registers 150 0F.

⇒ Transfer to a cutting board; let rest for 5 minutes.

⇒ Pour off any fat remaining in the pan (take care, the handle will still be hot); place the pan over medium-high heat and add orange juice and honey. Bring to a simmer, stirring to scrape up any browned bits.

⇒ Add orange zest and soy sauce and continue to cook until the sauce is slightly reduced, about 1 minute. Stir cornstarch mixture then whisk into the sauce; cook, stirring, until slightly thickened, 1 minute.

⇒ Remove the duck skin and thinly slice the breast meat. Drizzle with the orange sauce.

Nutrition: Calories: 152, Fat:2 g, Carbs:8 g, Protein:24 g, Sugars:5 g, Sodium:309 mg

53) Pork Chops With Tomato Salsa

Preparation Time: **Cooking Time: 15 Minutes**   **Servings:4**

Ingredients:

- 4 pork chops
- 1 tablespoon olive oil
- 4 scallions, chopped
- 1 teaspoon cumin, ground
- ½ tablespoon hot paprika
- 1 teaspoon garlic powder
- A pinch of sea salt and black pepper

- 1 small red onion, chopped
- 2 tomatoes, cubed
- 2 tablespoons lime juice
- 1 jalapeno, chopped
- ¼ cup cilantro, chopped
- 1 tablespoon lime juice

Directions:

⇒ Heat up a pan with the oil over medium heat, add the scallions and sauté for 5 minutes.

⇒ Add the meat, cumin paprika, garlic powder, salt and pepper, toss, cook for 5 minutes on each side and divide between plates.

⇒ In a bowl, combine the tomatoes with the remaining ingredients, toss, divide next to the pork chops and serve.

Nutrition: calories 313, fat 23.7, fiber 1.7, carbs 5.9, protein 19.2

54) Tuscan Chicken With Tomatoes, Olives, And Zucchini

Preparation Time: **Cooking Time: 20 Minutes**   **Servings:4**

Ingredients:

- 4 boneless, skinless chicken breast halves, pounded to ½- to ¾-inch thickness
- 1 teaspoon garlic powder
- ½ teaspoon sea salt
- ⅛ teaspoon freshly ground black pepper
- 2 tablespoons extra-virgin olive oil

- 2 cups cherry tomatoes
- ½ cup sliced green olives
- 1 zucchini, chopped
- ¼ cup dry white wine

Directions:

⇒ On a clean work surface, rub the chicken breasts with garlic powder, salt, and ground black pepper.

⇒ Heat the olive oil in a nonstick skillet over medium-high heat until shimmering.

⇒ Add the chicken and cook for 16 minutes or until the internal temperature reaches at least 165°F (74°C). Flip the chicken halfway through the cooking time. Transfer to a large plate and cover with aluminum foil to keep warm.

⇒ Add the tomatoes, olives, and zucchini to the skillet and sauté for 4 minutes or until the vegetables are soft.

⇒ Add the white wine to the skillet and simmer for 1 minutes.

⇒ Remove the aluminum foil and top the chicken with the vegetables and their juices, then serve warm.

Nutrition: calories: 172 ; fat: 11.1g ; protein: 8.2g ; carbs: 7.9g ; fiber: 2.1g ; sugar: 4.2g ; sodium: 742mg

55) Pork Salad

Preparation Time: **Cooking Time: 10 Minutes**   **Servings:4**

Ingredients:

- 1-pound pork stew meat, cut into strips
- 3 tablespoons olive oil
- 4 scallions, chopped
- 2 tablespoons lemon juice
- 2 tablespoons balsamic vinegar

- 2 cups mixed salad greens
- 1 avocado, peeled, pitted and roughly cubed
- 1 cucumber, sliced
- 2 tomatoes, cubed
- A pinch of salt and black pepper

Directions:

⇒ Heat up a pan with 2 tablespoons of oil over medium heat, add the scallions, the meat and the lemon juice, toss and cook for 10 minutes.

⇒ In a salad bowl, combine the salad greens with the meat and the remaining ingredients, toss and serve.

Nutrition: calories 225, fat 6.4, fiber 4, carbs 8, protein 11

56) Lime Pork And Green Beans

Preparation Time: **Cooking Time: 40 Minutes**   **Servings:4**

Ingredients:

- 2 pounds pork stew meat, cubed
- 2 tablespoons avocado oil
- ½ cup green beans, trimmed and halved
- 2 tablespoons lime juice

- 1 cup coconut milk
- 1 tablespoon rosemary, chopped
- A pinch of salt and black pepper

Directions:

⇒ Heat up a pan with the oil over medium heat, add the meat and brown for 5 minutes.

⇒ Add the rest of the ingredients, toss gently, bring to a simmer and cook over medium heat for 35 minutes more.

⇒ Divide the mix between plates and serve.

Nutrition: calories 260, fat 5, fiber 8, carbs 9, protein 13

57) Pork With Chili Zucchinis And Tomatoes

Preparation Time: **Cooking Time: 35 Minutes**   **Servings:4**

Ingredients:

- 2 tomatoes, cubed
- 2 pounds pork stew meat, cubed
- 4 scallions, chopped
- 2 tablespoons olive oil
- 1 zucchini, sliced

- Juice of 1 lime
- 2 tablespoons chili powder
- ½ tablespoons cumin powder
- A pinch of sea salt and black pepper

Directions:

⇒ Heat up a pan with the oil over medium heat, add the scallions and sauté for 5 minutes.

⇒ Add the meat and brown for 5 minutes more.

⇒ Add the tomatoes and the other ingredients, toss, cook over medium heat for 25 minutes more, divide between plates and serve.

Nutrition: calories 300, fat 5, fiber 2, carbs 12, protein 14

58) Pork With Olives

Preparation Time: **Cooking Time: 40 Minutes**   **Servings:4**

Ingredients:

- 1 yellow onion, chopped
- 4 pork chops
- 2 tablespoons olive oil
- 1 tablespoon sweet paprika
- 2 tablespoons balsamic vinegar

- ¼ cup kalamata olives, pitted and chopped
- 1 tablespoon cilantro, chopped
- A pinch of sea salt and black pepper

Directions:

⇒ Heat up a pan with the oil over medium heat, add the onion and sauté for 5 minutes.

⇒ Add the meat and brown for 5 minutes more.

⇒ Add the rest of the ingredients, toss, cook over medium heat for 30 minutes, divide between plates and serve.

Nutrition: calories 280, fat 11, fiber 6, carbs 10, protein 21

59) Pork With Nutmeg Squash

Preparation Time: **Cooking Time: 35 Minutes**   **Servings:4**

Ingredients:

- 1-pound pork stew meat, cubed
- 1 butternut squash, peeled and cubed
- 1 yellow onion, chopped
- 2 tablespoons olive oil
- 2 garlic cloves, minced

- ½ teaspoon garam masala
- ½ teaspoon nutmeg, ground
- 1 teaspoon chili flakes, crushed
- 1 tablespoon balsamic vinegar
- A pinch of sea salt and black pepper

Directions:

⇒ Heat up a pan with the oil over medium-high heat, add the onion and the garlic and sauté for 5 minutes.

⇒ Add the meat and brown for another 5 minutes.

⇒ Add the rest of the ingredients, toss, cook over medium heat for 25 minutes, divide between plates and serve.

Nutrition: calories 348, fat 18.2, fiber 2.1, carbs 11.4, protein 34.3

60) Creamy Pork And Tomatoes

| Preparation Time: | Cooking Time: 35 Minutes | Servings:4 |

Ingredients:

- 2 pounds pork stew meat, cubed
- 2 tablespoons avocado oil
- 1 cup tomatoes, cubed
- 1 cup coconut cream
- 1 tablespoon mint, chopped

- 1 jalapeno pepper, chopped
- A pinch of sea salt and black pepper
- 1 tablespoon hot pepper
- 2 tablespoons lemon juice

Directions:

⇒ Heat up a pan with the oil over medium heat, add the meat and brown for 5 minutes.

⇒ Add the rest of the ingredients, toss, cook over medium heat for 30 minutes more, divide between plates and serve.

Nutrition: calories 230, fat 4, fiber 6, carbs 9, protein 14

61) Lemon Tenderloin

| Preparation Time: | Cooking Time: 25 Minutes | Servings:2 |

Ingredients:

- ¼ teaspoon za'atar seasoning
- Zest of 1 lemon
- ½ teaspoon dried thyme
- ¼ teaspoon garlic powder

- ¼ teaspoon salt
- 1 tablespoon olive oil
- 1 (8-ounce / 227-g) pork tenderloin, sliver skin trimmed

Directions:

⇒ Preheat the oven to 425°F (220°C).

⇒ Combine the za'atar seasoning, lemon zest, thyme, garlic powder, and salt in a bowl, then rub the pork tenderloin with the mixture on both sides.

⇒ Warm the olive oil in an oven-safe skillet over medium-high heat until shimmering.

⇒ Add the pork tenderloin and sear for 6 minutes or until browned. Flip the pork halfway through the cooking time.

⇒ Arrange the skillet in the preheated oven and roast for 15 minutes or until an instant-read thermometer inserted in the thickest part of the tenderloin registers at least 145°F (63°C).

⇒ Transfer the cooked tenderloin to a large plate and allow to cool for a few minutes before serving.

Nutrition: calories: 184 ; fat: 10.8g ; carbs: 1.2g ; fiber: 0g ; protein: 20.1g ; sodium: 358mg

62) Chicken With Broccoli

| Preparation Time: | Cooking Time: | Servings:4 |

Ingredients:

- 1 chopped small white onion
- 1½ c. low-fat, low-sodium chicken broth
- Freshly ground black pepper

- 2 c. chopped broccoli
- 1 lb. cubed, skinless and de-boned chicken thighs
- 2 minced garlic cloves

Directions:

⇒ In a slow cooker, add all ingredients and mix well.

⇒ Set slow cooker on low.

⇒ Cover and cook for 4-5 hours.

⇒ Serve hot.

Nutrition: Calories: 300, Fat:9 g, Carbs:19 g, Protein:31 g, Sugars:6 g, Sodium:200 mg

63) Pork With Mushrooms And Cucumbers

Preparation Time:	Cooking Time: 25 Minutes	Servings:4

Ingredients:

- 2 tablespoons olive oil
- ½ teaspoon oregano, dried
- 4 pork chops
- 2 garlic cloves, minced
- Juice of 1 lime

- ¼ cup cilantro, chopped
- A pinch of sea salt and black pepper
- 1 cup white mushrooms, halved
- 2 tablespoons balsamic vinegar

Directions:

⇒ Heat up a pan with the oil over medium heat, add the pork chops and brown for 2 minutes on each side.

⇒ Add the rest of the ingredients, toss, cook over medium heat for 20 minutes, divide between plates and serve.

Nutrition: calories 220, fat 6, fiber 8, carbs 14.2, protein 20

64) Chicken Chopstick

Preparation Time:	Cooking Time:	Servings:4

Ingredients:

- ¼ c. diced chopped onion
- 1 pack cooked chow Mein noodles
- Fresh ground pepper
- 2 cans cream mushroom soup

- 1 ¼ c. sliced celery
- 1 c. cashew nuts
- 2 c. cubed cooked chicken
- ½ c. water

Directions:

⇒ 1 ¼ c. sliced celery

⇒ 1 c. cashew nuts

⇒ 2 c. cubed cooked chicken

⇒ ½ c. water

⇒ Add half the noodles to the mixture, stir until coated.

⇒ Top the casserole with the rest of the noodles.

⇒ Place the pot in the oven. Bake for 25 minutes.

⇒ Serve immediately.

Nutrition: Calories: 201, Fat:17 g, Carbs:15 g, Protein:13 g, Sugars:7 g, Sodium:10 mg

65) Balsamic Roast Chicken

Preparation Time:	Cooking Time:	Servings:4

Ingredients:

- 1 tbsp. minced fresh rosemary
- 1 minced garlic clove
- Black pepper
- 1 tbsp. olive oil

- 1 tsp. brown sugar
- 6 rosemary sprigs
- 1 whole chicken
- ½ c. balsamic vinegar

Directions:

⇒ Combine garlic, minced rosemary, black pepper and the olive oil. Rub the chicken with the herbal olive oil mixture.

⇒ Put 3 rosemary sprigs into the chicken cavity.

⇒ Place the chicken into a roasting pan and roast at 400F for about 1 hr. 30 minutes.

⇒ When the chicken is golden and the juices run clear, transfer to a serving dish.

⇒ In a saucepan dissolve the sugar in balsamic vinegar over heat. Do not boil.

⇒ Carve the chicken and top with vinegar mixture.

Nutrition: Calories: 587, Fat:37.8 g, Carbs:2.5 g, Protein:54.1 g, Sugars:0 g, Sodium:600 mg

66) Peach Chicken Treat

Preparation Time: **Cooking Time:**   **Servings: 4-5**

Ingredients:

- 2 minced garlic cloves
- ¼ c. balsamic vinegar
- 4 sliced peaches
- 4 skinless, deboned chicken breasts

- ¼ c. chopped basil
- 1 tbsp. olive oil
- 1 chopped shallot
- ¼ tsp. black pepper

Directions:

⇒ Heat up the oil in a saucepan over medium-high flame.

⇒ Add the meat and season with black pepper; fry for 8 minutes on each side and set aside to rest in a plate.

⇒ In the same pan, add the shallot and garlic; stir and cook for 2 minutes.

⇒ Add the peaches; stir and cook for 4-5 more minutes.

⇒ Add the vinegar, cooked chicken, and basil; toss and simmer covered for 3-4 minutes more.

⇒ Serve warm.

Nutrition: Calories: 270, Fat:0 g, Carbs:6.6 g, Protein:1.5 g, Sugars:24 g, Sodium:87 mg

67) Ground Pork Pan

Preparation Time: **Cooking Time: 15 Minutes**   **Servings:4**

Ingredients:

- 2 garlic cloves, minced
- 2 red chilies, chopped
- 2 tablespoons olive oil
- 2 pounds pork stew meat, ground
- 1 red bell pepper, chopped
- 1 green bell pepper, chopped

- 1 tomato, cubed
- ½ cup mushrooms, halved
- A pinch of sea salt and black pepper
- 1 tablespoon basil, chopped
- 2 tablespoons coconut aminos

Directions:

⇒ Heat up a pan with the oil over medium heat, add the garlic, chilies, bell peppers, tomato and the mushrooms and sauté for 5 minutes.

⇒ Add the meat and the rest of the ingredients, toss, cook over medium heat for 10 minutes more, divide between plates and serve.

Nutrition: calories 200, fat 3, fiber 5, carbs 7, protein 17

68) Parsley Pork And Artichokes

Preparation Time: **Cooking Time: 35 Minutes**   **Servings:4**

Ingredients:

- 2 tablespoons balsamic vinegar
- 1 cup canned artichoke hearts, drained and quartered
- 2 tablespoons olive oil
- 2 pounds pork stew meat, cubed
- 2 tablespoons parsley, chopped

- 1 teaspoon cumin, ground
- 1 teaspoon turmeric powder
- 2 garlic cloves, minced
- A pinch of sea salt and black pepper

Directions:

⇒ Heat up a pan with the oil over medium heat, add the meat and brown for 5 minutes.

⇒ Add the artichokes, the vinegar and the other ingredients, toss, cook over medium heat for 30 minutes, divide between plates and serve.

Nutrition: calories 260, fat 5, fiber 4, carbs 11, protein 20

69) Pork With Thyme Sweet Potatoes

Preparation Time: **Cooking Time: 35 Minutes**   **Servings:4**

Ingredients:

- 2 sweet potatoes, peeled and cut into wedges
- 4 pork chops
- 3 spring onions, chopped
- 1 tablespoon thyme, chopped
- 2 tablespoons olive oil

- 4 garlic cloves, minced
- A pinch of sea salt and black pepper
- ½ cup vegetable stock
- ½ tablespoon chives, chopped

Directions:

⇒ In a roasting pan, combine the pork chops with the potatoes and the other ingredients, toss gently and cook at 390 degrees F for 35 minutes.

⇒ Divide everything between plates and serve.

Nutrition: calories 210, fat 12.2, fiber 5.2, carbs 12, protein 10

70) Curry Pork Mix

Preparation Time: **Cooking Time: 30 Minutes**   **Servings:4**

Ingredients:

- 2 tablespoon olive oil
- 4 scallions, chopped
- 2 garlic cloves, minced
- 2 pounds pork stew meat, cubed
- 2 tablespoons red curry paste

- 1 teaspoon chili paste
- 2 tablespoons balsamic vinegar
- ¼ cup vegetable stock
- ¼ cup parsley, chopped

Directions:

⇒ Heat up a pan with the oil over medium-high heat, add the scallions and the garlic and sauté for 5 minutes.

⇒ Add the meat and brown for 5 minutes more.

⇒ Add the remaining ingredients, toss, cook over medium heat for 20 minutes, divide between plates and serve.

Nutrition: calories 220, fat 3, fiber 4, carbs 7, protein 12

71) Stir-fried Chicken And Broccoli

Preparation Time: **Cooking Time: 10 Minutes**   **Servings:4**

Ingredients:

- 3 tablespoons extra-virgin olive oil
- 1½ cups broccoli florets
- 1½ pounds (680 g) boneless, skinless chicken breasts, cut into bite-size pieces
- ½ onion, chopped

- ½ teaspoon sea salt
- ⅛ teaspoon freshly ground black pepper
- 3 garlic cloves, minced
- 2 cups cooked brown rice

Directions:

⇒ Heat the olive oil in a large nonstick skillet over medium-high heat until shimmering.

⇒ Add the broccoli, chicken, and onion to the skillet and stir well. Season with sea salt and black pepper.

⇒ Stir-fry for about 8 minutes, or until the chicken is golden browned and cooked through.

⇒ Toss in the garlic and cook for 30 seconds, stirring constantly, or until the garlic is fragrant.

⇒ Remove from the heat to a plate and serve over the cooked brown rice.

Nutrition: calories: 344 ; fat: 14.1g ; protein: 14.1g ; carbs: 40.9g ; fiber: 3.2g ; sugar: 1.2g ; sodium: 275mg

72) Chicken And Broccoli

Preparation Time: **Cooking Time:** **Servings:4**

Ingredients:

- 2 minced garlic cloves
- 4 de-boned, skinless chicken breasts
- ½ c. coconut cream
- 1 tbsp. chopped oregano

- 2 c. broccoli florets
- 1 tbsp. organic olive oil
- 1 c. chopped red onions

Directions:

⇒ Heat up a pan while using the oil over medium-high heat, add chicken breasts and cook for 5 minutes on each side.

⇒ Add onions and garlic, stir and cook for 5 minutes more.

⇒ Add oregano, broccoli and cream, toss everything, cook for ten minutes more, divide between plates and serve.

⇒ Enjoy!

Nutrition: Calories: 287, Fat:10 g, Carbs:14 g, Protein:19 g, Sugars:10 g, Sodium:1106 mg

73) Pork With Cabbage And Kale

Preparation Time: **Cooking Time: 35 Minutes** **Servings:4**

Ingredients:

- 1-pound pork stew meat, cut into strips
- 2 tablespoons olive oil
- 1 yellow onion, chopped
- A pinch of sea salt and black pepper
- cup green cabbage, shredded

- ½ cup baby kale
- 2 tablespoons oregano, dried
- 2 tablespoons balsamic vinegar
- ¼ cup vegetable stock

Directions:

⇒ Heat up a pan with the oil over medium-high heat, add the onion and the meat and brown for 5 minutes.

⇒ Add the cabbage and the other ingredients, toss gently and bake everything at 390 degrees F for 30 minutes.

⇒ Divide the whole mix between plates and serve.

Nutrition: calories 331, fat 18.7, fiber 2.1, carbs 6.5, protein 34.2

74) Mediterranean Chicken Bake With Vegetables

Preparation Time: **Cooking Time: 20 Minutes** **Servings:4**

Ingredients:

- 4 (4-ounce / 113-g) boneless, skinless chicken breasts
- 2 tablespoons avocado oil
- 1 cup sliced cremini mushrooms
- 1 cup packed chopped fresh spinach
- 1 pint cherry tomatoes, halved

- ½ cup chopped fresh basil
- ½ red onion, thinly sliced
- 4 garlic cloves, minced
- 2 teaspoons balsamic vinegar

Directions:

⇒ Preheat the oven to 400°F (205°C).

⇒ Arrange the chicken breast in a large baking dish and brush them generously with the avocado oil.

⇒ Mix together the mushrooms, spinach, tomatoes, basil, red onion, cloves, and vinegar in a medium bowl, and toss to combine. Scatter each chicken breast with ¼ of the vegetable mixture.

⇒ Bake in the preheated oven for about 20 minutes, or until the internal temperature reaches at least 165°F (74°C) and juices run clear when pierced with a fork.

⇒ Allow the chicken to rest for 5 to 10 minutes before slicing to serve.

Nutrition: calories: 220 ; fat: 9.1g ; protein: 28.2g ; carbs: 6.9g ; fiber: 2.1g ; sugar: 6.7g ; sodium: 310mg

75) Hidden Valley Chicken Drummies

Preparation Time: **Cooking Time:**   **Servings:6-8**

Ingredients:

- 2 tbsps. Hot sauce
- ½ c. melted butter
- Celery sticks
- 2 packages Hidden Valley dressing dry mix

- 3 tbsps. Vinegar
- 12 chicken drumsticks
- Paprika

Directions:

⇒ Preheat the oven to 350 0F.

⇒ Rinse and pat dry the chicken.

⇒ In a bowl blend the dry dressing, melted butter, vinegar and hot sauce. Stir until combined.

⇒ Place the drumsticks in a large plastic baggie, pour the sauce over drumsticks. Massage the sauce until the drumsticks are coated.

⇒ Place the chicken in a single layer on a baking dish. Sprinkle with paprika.

⇒ Bake for 30 minutes, flipping halfway.

⇒ Serve with crudité or salad.

Nutrition: Calories: 155, Fat:18 g, Carbs:96 g, Protein:15 g, Sugars:0.7 g, Sodium:340 mg

76) Balsamic Chicken And Beans

Preparation Time: **Cooking Time:**   **Servings: 4**

Ingredients:

- 1 lb. trimmed fresh green beans
- ¼ c. balsamic vinegar
- 2 sliced shallots
- 2 tbsps. Red pepper flakes

- 4 skinless, de-boned chicken breasts
- 2 minced garlic cloves
- 3 tbsps. Extra virgin olive oil

Directions:

⇒ Combine 2 tablespoons of the olive oil with the balsamic vinegar, garlic, and shallots. Pour it over the chicken breasts and refrigerate overnight.

⇒ The next day, preheat the oven to 375 0F.

⇒ Take the chicken out of the marinade and arrange in a shallow baking pan. Discard the rest of the marinade.

⇒ Bake in the oven for 40 minutes.

⇒ While the chicken is cooking, bring a large pot of water to a boil.

⇒ Place the green beans in the water and allow them to cook for five minutes and then drain.

⇒ Heat one tablespoon of olive oil in the pot and return the green beans after rinsing them.

⇒ Toss with red pepper flakes.

Nutrition: Calories: 433, Fat:17.4 g, Carbs:12.9 g, Protein:56.1 g, Sugars:13 g, Sodium:292 mg

77) Italian Pork

Preparation Time: **Cooking Time: 1 Hour**   **Servings:6**

Ingredients:

- 2 pounds pork roast
- 3 tablespoons olive oil
- 2 teaspoons oregano, dried
- 1 tablespoon Italian seasoning
- 1 teaspoon rosemary, dried

- 1 teaspoon basil, dried
- 3 garlic cloves, minced
- ¼ cup vegetable stock
- A pinch of salt and black pepper

Directions:

⇒ In a baking pan, combine the pork roast with the oil, the oregano and the other ingredients, toss and bake at 390 degrees F for 1 hour.

⇒ Slice the roast, divide it and the other ingredients between plates and serve.

Nutrition: calories 580, fat 33.6, fiber 0.5, carbs 2.3, protein 64.9

78) Chicken And Brussels Sprouts

Preparation Time: **Cooking Time:** **Servings:4**

Ingredients:

- 1 cored, peeled and chopped apple
- 1 chopped yellow onion
- 1 tbsp. organic olive oil
- 3 c. shredded Brussels sprouts
- 1 lb. ground chicken meat
- Black pepper

Directions:

⇒ Heat up a pan while using oil over medium-high heat, add chicken, stir and brown for 5 minutes.

⇒ Enjoy!

⇒ Add Brussels sprouts, onion, black pepper and apple, stir, cook for 10 minutes, divide into bowls and serve.

Nutrition: Calories: 200, Fat:8 g, Carbs:13 g, Protein:9 g, Sugars:3.3 g, Sodium:194 mg

79) Chicken Divan

Preparation Time: **Cooking Time:** **Servings:**

Ingredients:

- 1 c. croutons
- 1 c. cooked and diced broccoli pieces
- ½ c. water
- 1 c. grated extra sharp cheddar cheese
- ½ lb. de-boned and skinless cooked chicken pieces
- 1 can mushroom soup

Directions:

⇒ Preheat the oven to 350∘F

⇒ In a large pot, heat the soup and water. Add the chicken, broccoli, and cheese. Combine thoroughly.

⇒ Pour into a greased baking dish.

⇒ Place the croutons over the mixture.

⇒ Bake for 30 minutes or until the casserole is bubbling and the croutons are golden brown.

Nutrition: Calories: 380, Fat:22 g, Carbs:10 g, Protein:25 g, Sugars:2 g, Sodium:475 mg

Snack & Dessert Recipes

80) Boiled Cabbage

Preparation Time: **Cooking Time: 5 Minutes**   **Servings:6**

Ingredients:

- 1 large head green cabbage
- 3 cups vegetable broth

- 1 teaspoon salt
- ½ teaspoon black pepper

Directions:

⇒ Place the cabbage, broth, salt, and pepper in the inner pot.   ⇒ Cook within 5 minutes. Serve.

Nutrition: Calories 54Fat: 0gProtein: 3gSodium: 321mgFiber: 5gCarbohydrates: 13gSugar: 7g

81) Cereal Mix

Preparation Time: **Cooking Time: 40 Minutes**   **Servings:6**

Ingredients:

- 3 tablespoons extra virgin organic olive oil
- 1 teaspoon hot sauce
- ½ teaspoon garlic powder
- ½ teaspoon onion powder
- ½ teaspoon cumin, ground

- A pinch of red pepper cayenne
- 3 cups rice cereal squares
- 1 cup cornflakes
- ½ cup pepitas

Directions:

⇒ In a bowl, combine the oil while using the hot sauce, garlic powder, onion powder, cumin, cayenne, rice cereal, cornflakes and pepitas.

⇒ Toss and spread on the lined baking sheet.

⇒ Put inside the oven and bake at 350 degrees F for 40 minutes.

⇒ Divide into bowls and serve as a snack.

Nutrition: Calories: 199Fat: 3gFiber: 4gCarbs: 12g Protein: 5g

82) Steamed Broccoli

Preparation Time: **Cooking Time: 1 Minute**   **Servings:6**

Ingredients:

- 6 cups broccoli florets

Directions:

⇒ Pour 1½ cups water into the inner pot of the Instant Pot®. Place a steam rack inside.

⇒ Place the broccoli florets inside a steamer basket and place the basket on the steam rack.

⇒ Steam within 1 minute.

⇒ Remove the steamer basket and serve.

Nutrition: Calories 30Fat: 0gProtein: 3gSodium: 30mgFiber: 2gCarbohydrates: 6gSugar: 2g

83) Berries Cream

Preparation Time: **Cooking Time: 15 Minutes**   **Servings:4**

Ingredients:

- 2 teaspoons lemon juice
- 1-pound blueberries

- 1-pound strawberries

Directions:

⇒ In a small pot, mix the lemon juice with the strawberries and blueberries. Stir, bring to a simmer over medium heat, cook for 15 minutes, divide into bowls and serve cold.

⇒ Enjoy!

Nutrition: calories 132, fat 2, fiber 3, carbs 8, protein 5

84) Turmeric Bars

Preparation Time: **Cooking Time: 10 Minutes**   **Servings:6**

Ingredients:

- 1 cup shredded coconut
- 10 dates, pitted
- 1 tablespoon coconut oil
- 1 teaspoon cinnamon

- 1 ¼ cup coconut butter
- 1 ½ teaspoon turmeric powder
- 2 teaspoons honey
- 1/8 teaspoon black pepper

Directions:

⇒ Prepare a baking pan and line with parchment paper.

⇒ Place the coconut and dates in a food processor and pulse until well-combined. Add in the coconut oil and cinnamon.

⇒ Press the dough at the bottom of the pan and set in the fridge for 2 hours.

⇒ Make the filling by melting the coconut butter in a double boiler. Stir in turmeric powder and honey.

⇒ Pour in the mixture into the pan with the crust.

⇒ Chill within 2 hours.

Nutrition: Calories 410 Total Fat 41g Total Carbs 13g Protein 1g Sugar: 11g Fiber: 2g Sodium: 208mg Potassium 347mg

85) Cinnamon Apple Mix

Preparation Time: **Cooking Time: 20 Minutes**   **Servings:6**

Ingredients:

- 6 apples, cored and roughly chopped
- 4 tablespoons chicory root powder
- 2 teaspoons vanilla extract

- 3 drops lemon oil
- 1 ½ teaspoon ground cinnamon

Directions:

⇒ In a small pot, mix the apples with chicory powder, vanilla, lemon oil and cinnamon. Stir and bring to a simmer over medium heat. Cook for 20 minutes then divide into bowls and serve cold.

⇒ Enjoy!

Nutrition: calories 110, fat 2, fiber 3, carbs 5, protein 5

86) Potato Chips

Preparation Time: **Cooking Time: 30 Minutes**   **Servings:6**

Ingredients:

- 2 gold potatoes, cut into thin rounds
- 1 tablespoon olive oil

- 2 teaspoons garlic, minced

Directions:

⇒ In a bowl, combine the French fries while using the oil along with the garlic, toss, spread more than a lined baking sheet.

⇒ Put inside the oven and bake at 400 degrees F for a half-hour.

⇒ Divide into bowls and serve.

Nutrition: Calories: 200,Fat: 3,Fiber: 5,Carbs: 13,Protein: 6

87) Piquillo Peppers With Cheese

Preparation Time:	Cooking Time: 10 Minutes	Servings: 24

Ingredients:

- 1 canned roasted piquillo peppers
- 2 tbsp olive oil
- 1 tbsp parsley, chopped
- Filling

- 2 oz. goat cheese
- 2 tbsp heavy cream
- 1 tbsp olive oil

Directions:

⇒ Prepare and set up the oven at 370 degrees F.

⇒ Layer a baking tray with some olive oil.

⇒ Whisk all goat cheese with cream and olive oil in a bowl.

⇒ Deseed the peppers and divide the cheese filling into each pepper.

⇒ Place them in the baking tray and drizzle the remaining oil and parsley on top.

⇒ Bake for 10 minutes then serve.

Nutrition: Calories 274 Fat 24.3g, Carbs 4.2g, Protein 11g, Fiber 2g

88) Lemon Garlic Red Chard

Preparation Time:	Cooking Time: 7 Minutes	Servings:4

Ingredients:

- 1 tablespoon avocado oil
- 1 small yellow onion, peeled and diced
- 1 bunch red chard, leaves and stems chopped and kept separate (about 12 ounces)
- 3 cloves garlic, minced

- ¾ teaspoon salt
- Juice from ½ medium lemon
- 1 teaspoon lemon zest

Directions:

⇒ Put the oil to the inner pot and allow it to heat 1 minute. Add the onion and chard stems and sauté 5 minutes. Put the garlic and sauté another 30 seconds. Put the chard leaves, salt, and lemon juice and stir to combine. Turn off. Cook again within 60 seconds.

⇒ Scoop the chard mixture into a serving bowl and top with lemon zest.

Nutrition: Calories 57Fat: 3gProtein: 2gSodium: 617mgFiber: 2gCarbohydrates: 6gSugar: 2g

89) Rice Pudding

Preparation Time:	Cooking Time: 35 Minutes	Servings:4

Ingredients:

- 6 cups almond milk
- Chicory root powder to the taste
- 2 cups black rice, washed and rinsed

- 1 tablespoon ground cinnamon
- ½ cup shredded coconut, unsweetened

Directions:

⇒ In a pot, mix the rice with the milk, chicory powder, cinnamon and coconut. Bring to a simmer over medium-low heat, cook for 35 minutes, divide into bowls to chill then serve cold.

⇒ Enjoy!

Nutrition: calories 170, fat 4, fiber 4, carbs 13, protein 6

90) Lemony Steamed Asparagus

Preparation Time: **Cooking Time: 0 Minutes**   **Servings:4**

Ingredients:

- 1-pound asparagus, woody ends removed
- Juice from ½ large lemon
- ¼ teaspoon kosher salt

Directions:

⇒ Add ½ cup water to the inner pot and add the steam rack. Add the asparagus to the steamer basket and place the basket on top of the rack, then steam within 1 minute.

⇒ Transfer, and top with lemon juice and salt.

Nutrition: Calories 13Fat: 0gProtein: 1gSodium: 146mgFiber: 1gCarbohydrates: 3gSugar: 1g

91) Fresh Veggie Bars

Preparation Time: **Cooking Time: 25 Minutes**   **Servings:18**

Ingredients:

- Egg-1
- Broccoli florets-2 cups
- Cheddar cheese-1/3 cup (grated)
- Onion-¼ cup (peeled and chopped)
- Cauliflower rice-½ cup
- Fresh parsley-2 tablespoons (chopped)
- Olive oil-A drizzle (for greasing)
- Salt and black pepper-to taste (ground)

Directions:

⇒ Warm-up a saucepan with water over medium heat

⇒ Stir into the broccoli and let it simmer for a minute.

⇒ Strain and finely chop it to put it into a bowl.

⇒ Mix in the egg, cheddar cheese, cauliflower rice, salt, pepper, parsley, and mix.

⇒ Give them the shape of bars by using the mixture on your hands.

⇒ Put them on a greased baking sheet.

⇒ Keep it in an oven at 400°F and bake for 20 minutes.

⇒ Settle the prepared dish on a platter to serve.

Nutrition: Calories: 19Fat: 1g Fiber: 3gCarbs: 3gProtein: 3g

92) "cheesy" Brussels Sprouts And Carrots

Preparation Time: **Cooking Time: 10 Minutes**   **Servings:4**

Ingredients:

- 1-pound Brussels sprouts, tough ends removed and cut in half
- 1-pound baby carrots
- 1 cup chicken stock
- 2 tablespoons lemon juice
- ½ cup nutritional yeast
- ¼ teaspoon salt

Directions:

⇒ Add the Brussels sprouts, carrots, stock, lemon juice, nutritional yeast, and salt to the inner pot. Stir well to combine. Cook within 10 minutes.

⇒ Transfer the vegetables and sauce to a bowl and serve.

Nutrition: Calories 134Fat: 1gProtein: 9gSodium: 340mgFiber: 8gCarbohydrates: 23gSugar: 8g

93) Simple Banana Cake

Preparation Time: **Cooking Time: 45 Minutes** **Servings:4**

Ingredients:

- 1 ½ cups stevia
- 2 cups almond flour
- 3 bananas, peeled and mashed
- 3 eggs

- 2 teaspoon baking powder
- 1 teaspoon ground cinnamon
- 1 teaspoon ground nutmeg

Directions:

⇒ In a bowl, mix the eggs with the stevia, baking powder, cinnamon, nutmeg, banana and flour. Stir well and pour into a greased cake pan then cover with tin foil.

⇒ Place the pan in the oven, bake at 350 degrees F for 45 minutes then let the cake cool, slice and serve.

⇒ Enjoy!

Nutrition: calories 300, fat 11, fiber 11, carbs 12, protein 4

94) Massaged Kale Chips

Preparation Time: **Cooking Time: 20 Minutes** **Servings:2 cups**

Ingredients:

- 4 cups kale, stemmed, rinsed, drained, torn into 2-inch pieces
- 2 tablespoons extra-virgin olive oil

- 1 teaspoon sea salt
- 2 tablespoons apple cider vinegar

Directions:

⇒ Preheat the oven to 350°F (180°C).

⇒ Combine all the ingredients in a large bowl. Stir to mix well.

⇒ Gently massage the kale leaves in the bowl for 5 minutes or until wilted and bright.

⇒ Place the kale on a baking sheet. Bake in the preheated oven for 20 minutes or until crispy. Toss the kale halfway through.

⇒ Remove the kale from the oven and serve immediately.

Nutrition: (1 cup)calories: 138 ; fat: 13.8g ; protein: 1.4g ; carbs: 2.9g ; fiber: 1.2g ; sugar: 0.8g ; sodium: 1176mg

95) Orange And Blackberry Cream

Preparation Time: **Cooking Time: 20 Minutes** **Servings:6**

Ingredients:

- 5 tablespoons chicory root powder
- 1-ounce orange juice

- 1 pound blackberries

Directions:

⇒ In a pot, mix the blackberries with the orange juice and chicory powder. Stir and bring to a simmer over medium heat.

⇒ Cook for 20 minutes, divide into bowls and serve cold.

⇒ Enjoy!

Nutrition: calories 110, fat 2, fiber 3, carbs 6, protein 6

96) Lemon Ginger Broccoli And Carrots

Preparation Time: **Cooking Time: 5 Minutes** **Servings:6**

Ingredients:

- 1 tablespoon avocado oil
- 1" fresh ginger, peeled and thinly sliced
- 1 clove garlic, minced
- 2 broccoli crowns, florets

- 2 large carrots, sliced
- ½ teaspoon kosher salt
- Juice from ½ large lemon
- ¼ cup of water

Directions:

⇒ Put the oil to the inner pot. Heat-up within 2 minutes.

⇒ Add the ginger and garlic and sauté 1 minute. Add the broccoli, carrots, and salt and stir to combine. Turn off.

⇒ Add the lemon juice and water and use a wooden spoon to scrape up any brown bits—Cook within 2 minutes.

⇒ Serve immediately.

Nutrition: Calories 67Fat: 2gProtein: 3gSodium: 245mgFiber: 3gCarbohydrates: 10gSugar: 3g

97) Lemony Cauliflower Rice

Preparation Time: **Cooking Time: 8 Minutes**   **Servings:4**

Ingredients:

- 1 tablespoon avocado oil
- 1 small yellow onion, peeled and diced
- 1 teaspoon minced garlic
- 4 cups riced cauliflower
- Juice from 1 little lemon
- ½ teaspoon salt
- ¼ teaspoon black pepper

Directions:

⇒ Put the oil to the pot, and heat 1 minute.

⇒ Add the onion and sauté 5 minutes.

⇒ Add the garlic and sauté 1 more minute.

⇒ Add the cauliflower rice, lemon juice, salt, and pepper and stir to combine—Cook within 1 minute.

⇒ Transfer to a bowl for serving.

Nutrition: Calories 60Fat: 3gProtein: 2gSodium: 311mgFiber: 2gCarbohydrates: 6gSugar: 3g

98) Peppers Avocado Salsa

Preparation Time: **Cooking Time: 12 Minutes**   **Servings:2**

Ingredients:

- 1 and ½ lbs. mixed bell peppers, cut into strips
- 1 tablespoon avocado oil
- ½ cup tomato passata
- 1 avocado, peeled, pitted, and cubed
- Salt and black pepper, to taste

Directions:

⇒ Add bell peppers and all other ingredients to a suitable cooking pot.

⇒ Cover the pot's lid and cook for 12 minutes on medium heat.

⇒ Serve fresh and enjoy.

Nutrition: Calories 304Total Fat 20 g Cholesterol 12 mg Sodium 645 mg Total Carbs 9 g Sugar 2 gFiber 5 g Protein 22 g

99) Cacao Brownies

Preparation Time: **Cooking Time: 3 Hours**   **Servings:4**

Ingredients:

- 3 tablespoons coconut oil, divided
- 1 cup almond butter
- 1 cup unsweetened cacao powder
- ½ cup coconut sugar
- 2 large eggs
- 2 ripe bananas
- 2 teaspoons vanilla extract
- 1 teaspoon baking soda
- ½ teaspoon sea salt

Directions:

⇒ Coat the bottom of the slow cooker with 1 tablespoon of coconut oil.

⇒ In a medium bowl, combine the almond butter, cacao powder, coconut sugar, eggs, bananas, vanilla, baking soda, and salt

⇒ Mash the bananas and stir well until a batter forms

⇒ Pour the batter into the slow cooker.

⇒ Cover the cooker and set to low. Cook for 2½ to 3 hours, until firm to a light touch but still gooey in the middle, and serve.

Nutrition:

Special
Recipes

100) Caesar Dressing

Preparation Time: **Cooking Time: 0 Minutes**   **Servings:2**

Ingredients:

- ¼ Cup Paleo mayonnaise
- 2 Tablespoons Olive Oil
- 2 Cloves Garlic, Minced
- ½ Teaspoon Anchovy Paste
- 1 Tablespoon White Wine Vinegar
- ½ Teaspoon Lemon Zest
- 2 Tablespoons Lemon Juice, Fresh
- Sea Salt & Black Pepper to Taste

Directions:

⇒ Whisk all of your ingredients together. It should be emulsified and combined.

⇒ Put salt and pepper, and then refrigerate it for up to a week.

Nutrition: Calories 167Protein: 0.2 Grams Fat: 18.9 Grams Carbs: 1.3 Grams

101) Massaged Kale And Crispy Chickpea Salad

Preparation Time: **Cooking Time: 15 Minutes**   **Servings:4-6**

Ingredients:

- 1 large bunch kale, rinsed, stemmed, and cut into thin strips
- 2 teaspoons freshly squeezed lemon juice
- 2 tablespoons extra-virgin olive oil, divided
- ¾ teaspoon sea salt, divided
- 1 (14-ounce / 397-g) can cooked chickpeas (about 2 cups)
- 1 teaspoon sweet paprika
- 1 avocado, chopped

Directions:

⇒ Put the kale in a large bowl, then drizzle with 1 tablespoon of olive oil and lemon juice. Sprinkle with ¼ teaspoon of salt.

⇒ Gently knead the kale leaves in the bowl for 5 minutes or until wilted and bright. Rip the leafy part of the kale off the stem, then discard the stem.

⇒ Heat the remaining olive oil in a nonstick skillet over medium-low heat until shimmering.

⇒ Add the chickpeas, paprika, and remaining salt, then cook for 15 minutes or until the chickpeas are crispy.

⇒ Transfer the kale to a large serving bowl, then top with chickpeas and avocado. Toss to combine well and serve.

Nutrition: calories: 359 ; fat: 20.0g ; protein: 13.0g ; carbs: 35.0g ; fiber: 10.0g ; sugars: 1.0g ; sodium: 497mg

102) Garlic Aioli

Preparation Time: **Cooking Time: 0 Minute**   **Servings:4**

Ingredients:

- ½ Cup anti-inflammatory mayonnaise (here)
- 3 garlic cloves, finely minced

Directions:

⇒ In a small bowl, whisk the mayonnaise and garlic to combine.

⇒ Keep refrigerated in a tightly sealed container for up to 4 days.

Nutrition: Calories: 169Total Fat: 20gTotal Carbs: <1gSugar: 0gFiber: 0gProtein: <1gSodium: 36mg

103) *Kamut*

Preparation Time: **Cooking Time: 15 Minutes**   **Servings:6**

Ingredients:

- 1 cup Kamut berries
- 2 cups water
- 1 teaspoon salt
- 1 onion

- 1 teaspoon turmeric
- 1 teaspoon cilantro
- 1 tablespoon cashew butter

Directions:

⇒ In a large pan, combine the Kamut berries and water together.

⇒ Add salt and close the lid.

⇒ Cook the dish for 50 minutes on the medium heat.

⇒ Meanwhile, peel the onion and chop it into small pieces.

⇒ Combine the chopped onion with the cilantro and turmeric. Stir the mixture.

⇒ Heat a pan and add the cashew butter.

⇒ Add the chopped onion mixture and sauté it for 5 minutes or until the onion is soft.

⇒ When Kamut berries are cooked, remove them from the heat and combine them with the chopped onion mixture.

⇒ Stir it carefully.

⇒ Serve the dish warm.

Nutrition: calories: 149, fat: 0.8g, total carbs: 24.2g, sugars: 0.8g, protein: 4.4g

104) *Salmon & Beans Salad*

Preparation Time: **Cooking Time: 7 Minutes**   **Servings:4**

Ingredients:

- For Salmon:
- 4 (6-ounce) salmon fillets
- Ground cumin, to taste
- Salt and freshly ground black pepper, to taste
- 2 tablespoons olive oil
- For Salad:
- 1 (15-ounce) can pinto beans, rinsed and drained

- 1 (15-ounce) can kidney beans, rinsed and drained
- 1 (15-ounce) can navy beans, rinsed and drained
- 1 medium bunch scallion, chopped
- 1 small bunch fresh parsley, chopped
- 1/3 cup extra-virgin essential olive oil
- ¼ cup freshly squeezed lemon juice
- Salt and freshly ground black pepper, to taste

Directions:

⇒ Sprinkle the salmon fillets with cumin, salt and black pepper evenly.

⇒ In a sizable nonstick skillet, heat oil on medium heat.

⇒ Ass salmon, skin-side down and cook for about 3-4 minutes.

⇒ Carefully flip the side and cook for about 3 minutes.

⇒ Meanwhile in the bowl, mix together all salad ingredients.

⇒ Top with salmon fillets and serve.

Nutrition: Calories: 429, Fat: 16g, Carbohydrates: 24g, Fiber: 2g, Protein: 40g

105) *Spinach Salad With Lemony Dressing*

Preparation Time: **Cooking Time: 0 Minutes**   **Servings:4**

Ingredients:

- 2 tablespoons freshly squeezed lemon juice
- ¼ cup Dijon mustard
- 1½ tablespoons maple syrup

- 2 tablespoons extra-virgin olive oil
- ¼ teaspoon sea salt, or to taste
- 6 cups baby spinach leaves

Directions:

⇒ Make the lemon dressing: Combine all the ingredients, except for the spinach, in a small bowl. Stir to mix well.

⇒ Put the spinach in a large serving bowl, the drizzle with the lemon dressing. Toss to combine well. Serve immediately.

Nutrition: calories: 150 ; fat: 14.0g ; protein: 2.0g ; carbs: 8.0g ; fiber: 2.0g ; sugars: 5.0g ; sodium: 362mg

106) Tender Amaranth Cutlets

Preparation Time: **Cooking Time: 15 Minutes**   **Servings:5**

Ingredients:

- 1 cup amaranth, cooked
- 1 teaspoon salt
- 1 egg, whisked
- 2 oz Parmesan
- 1 onion
- 1 tablespoon olive oil
- 1 teaspoon dill
- 1 teaspoon minced garlic
- ½ teaspoon lemon zest

Directions:

⇒ Peel the onion and dice it.

⇒ Heat a skillet and add the olive oil.

⇒ Put the diced onion in the skillet and cook for 5 minutes over medium heat. Stir the mixture frequently.

⇒ In a large bowl, combine the egg, cooked amaranth, onion, minced garlic, salt, and lemon zest.

⇒ Sprinkle the mixture with the dill and stir it carefully until you get a smooth mix.

⇒ Preheat the oven to 350 F.

⇒ Make small balls from the amaranth mixture and flatten them slightly.

⇒ Cover a tray with baking paper and transfer the amaranth balls to the tray.

⇒ Put the tray in the oven and cook the cutlets for 10 minutes.

⇒ When the cutlets are cooked, remove them from the oven and cool them a little.

⇒ Serve the dish immediately.

Nutrition: calories: 276, fat: 6.0g, total carbs: 29.9g, sugars: 1.7g, protein: 21.6g

107) Zoodle Bolognese

Preparation Time: **Cooking Time: 35 Minutes**   **Servings:4**

Ingredients:

- Bolognese
- 3 oz. olive oil
- 1 white onion, chopped
- 1 garlic clove, minced
- 3 oz. celery, chopped
- 3 cups crumbled tofu
- 2 tbsp tomato paste
- 1 ½ cups crushed tomatoes
- 1 tsp salt
- ¼ tsp black pepper
- 1 tbsp dried basil
- 1 tbsp Worcestershire sauce
- Water as needed
- Zoodles
- 2 lbs zucchini
- 2 tbsp butter
- Salt orblack pepper to taste

Directions:

⇒ Pour the olive oil into a saucepan and heat over medium heat. When no longer shimmering, add the onion, garlic, and celery. Sauté for 3 minutes or until the onions are soft and the carrots caramelized.

⇒ Pour in the tofu, tomato paste, tomatoes, salt, black pepper, basil, and Worcestershire sauce. Stir and cook for 15 minutes, or simmer for 30 minutes.

⇒ Mix in some water if the mixture is too thick and simmer further for 20 minutes.

⇒ While the sauce cooks, make the zoodles. Run the zucchini through a spiralizer to form noodles.

⇒ Melt the butter in a skillet over medium heat and toss the zoodles quickly in the butter, about 1 minute only.

⇒ Season with salt and black pepper.

⇒ Divide the zoodles into serving plates and spoon the Bolognese on top. Serve the dish immediately.

Nutrition: Calories:457, Total Fat:37g, Saturated Fat:8.1g, Total Carbs:17g, Dietary Fiber:5g, Sugar:4g, Protein:22g, Sodium:656mg

108) Stir-fry Sauce

Preparation Time: **Cooking Time: 0 Minute** **Servings:4**

Ingredients:

- ¼ Cup low-sodium soy sauce
- 3 garlic cloves, minced
- Juice of 2 limes
- 1 tablespoon grated fresh ginger
- 1 tablespoon arrowroot powder

Directions:

⇒ In a small bowl, whisk together the soy sauce, garlic, lime juice, ginger, and arrowroot powder.

Nutrition: Calories: 24Total Carbs: 4gSugar: 2gProtein: 1gSodium: 887mg

109) Chicken & Cabbage Salad

Preparation Time: **Cooking Time: 12 Minutes** **Servings:4**

Ingredients:

- For Chicken Marinade:
- ¼ cup scallion, chopped
- 2 tablespoons fresh ginger, minced
- ¼ cup coconut aminos
- ¼ cup olive oil
- 1 tablespoon honey
- Salt and freshly ground black pepper, to taste
- 2 skinless, boneless chicken breasts
- For Salad:
- ¼ cup balsamic vinegar
- 2 cups red cabbage, shredded
- 1 cup green cabbage, shredded
- 2 cups carrots, peeled and shredded
- 4 cups fresh kale, trimmed and chopped
- 3 scallions, chopped

Directions:

⇒ For chicken in a very bowl, mix together all ingredients except chicken.

⇒ In another bowl, coat chicken with 3 tablespoons of marinade.

⇒ Refrigerate to marinate approximately 30-60 minutes.

⇒ For dressing in a very bowl, mix together remaining marinade and vinegar.

⇒ Preheat the grill to medium-high heat. Grease the grill grate.

⇒ Remove chicken from refrigerator and discard any excess marinade.

⇒ Grill for about 5-6 minutes per side.

⇒ Remove from grill whilst aside to cool down the slightly.

⇒ Cut the chicken breasts in thin slices.

⇒ In a large serving bowl, mix together salad ingredients.

⇒ Add dressing and toss to coat well.

⇒ Top with chicken slices and serve.

Nutrition: Calories: 401, Fat: 6g, Carbohydrates: 29g, Fiber: 14g, Protein: 36g

110) Green Beans With Nuts

Preparation Time: **Cooking Time:** **Servings:2**

Ingredients:

- 3 minced garlic cloves
- 1 tbsp. olive oil
- ½ c. chopped walnuts
- 2 c. sliced green beans

Directions:

⇒ Boil the beans in salted water until tender.

⇒ Place the beans, garlic and walnuts in a preheated pan and cook for about 5-7 minutes on the stove.

Nutrition: Calories: 285, Fat:24.1 g, Carbs:7.1 g, Protein:10 g, Sugars:3.3 g, Sodium:311 mg

111) *Green Beans And Mushroom Sauté*

Preparation Time: **Cooking Time: 25 Minutes**   **Servings:6**

Ingredients:

- 1 pound green beans, trimmed
- 8 ounces white mushrooms, sliced
- 1 yellow onion, chopped

- 2 tablespoons olive oil
- ½ cup veggie stock
- A pinch of salt and black pepper

Directions:

⇒ Heat up a big pan with the oil over medium-high heat and add the onion, stir and cook for 4 minutes.

⇒ Add the stock and the mushrooms, then stir and cook for 6 minutes more.

⇒ Add green beans, salt and pepper.

⇒ Toss and cook over medium heat for 15 minutes, then divide everything between plates and serve as a side dish.

Nutrition: Calories 182Fat 4gFiber 5gCarbs 6gProtein 8g

112) *Endives And Broccoli*

Preparation Time: **Cooking Time: 20 Minutes**   **Servings:4**

Ingredients:

- 2 endives, shredded
- 1 cup broccoli florets
- 2 tablespoons olive oil
- 1 tablespoon walnuts, chopped
- 1 tablespoon almonds, chopped

- 2 garlic cloves, minced
- 1 teaspoon rosemary, dried
- 1 teaspoon cumin, ground
- 1 teaspoon chili powder

Directions:

⇒ In a roasting pan, combine the endives with the broccoli and the other ingredients, toss and bake at 380 degrees F for 20 minutes.

⇒ Divide the mix between plates and serve.

Nutrition: calories 139, fat 9.8, fiber 9.3, carbs 11.9, protein 4.9

113) *Beets Stewed With Apples*

Preparation Time: **Cooking Time:**   **Servings:2**

Ingredients:

- 2 tbsps. Tomato paste
- 1 tbsps. Olive oil
- 1 c. water

- 2 peeled, cored and sliced apples
- 3 peeled, boiled and grated beets
- 2 tbsps. Sour cream

Directions:

⇒ Boil the beets until half-done

⇒ In a deep pan preheated with olive oil cook the grated beets for 15 minutes.

⇒ Add the sliced apples, tomato paste, sour cream and 1 cup water. Stew for 30 minutes covered.

Nutrition: Calories: 346, Fat:7.7 g, Carbs:26.8 g, Protein:2 g, Sugars:10.2 g, Sodium:96.1 mg

114) Herbed Green Beans

Preparation Time: **Cooking Time:**   **Servings:4**

Ingredients:

- ½ c. chopped fresh mint
- 2 minced garlic cloves
- 1 tsp. lemon zest
- 4 c. trimmed green beans

- 1 tbsp. olive oil
- 1 tsp. coarse ground black pepper
- ½ c. chopped fresh parsley

Directions:

⇒ Heat the olive oil in a large sauté pan over medium heat. Add the green beans and garlic.

⇒ Sauté until the green beans are crisp tender, approximately 5-6 minutes.

⇒ Add the mint, parsley, lemon zest, and black pepper. Toss to coat.

⇒ Serve immediately.

Nutrition: Calories: 66.2, Fat:3.5 g, Carbs:8.3 g, Protein:2.1 g, Sugars:2 g, Sodium:65 mg

115) Peanut Sauce

Preparation Time: **Cooking Time: 0 Minute**   **Servings:8**

Ingredients:

- 1 cup lite coconut milk
- ¼ cup creamy peanut butter
- ¼ cup freshly squeezed lime juice

- 3 garlic cloves, minced
- 2 tablespoons low-sodium soy sauce, or gluten-free soy sauce, or tamari
- 1 tablespoon grated fresh ginger

Directions:

⇒ In a blender or food processor, process the coconut milk, peanut butter, lime juice, garlic, soy sauce, and ginger until smooth.

⇒ Keep refrigerated in a tightly sealed container for up to 5 days.

Nutrition: Calories: 143Total Fat: 11gTotal Carbs: 8gSugar: 2gFiber: 1gProtein: 6gSodium: 533mg

116) Walnut Pesto

Preparation Time: **Cooking Time: 0 Minute**   **Servings:8**

Ingredients:

- ½ Cup walnuts
- ¼ cup extra-virgin olive oil
- 4 garlic cloves, minced

- 1 cup baby spinach
- ¼ cup basil leaves
- ½ teaspoon sea salt

Directions:

⇒ In a blender or food processor, combine the walnuts, olive oil, garlic, spinach, basil, and salt.

⇒ Pulse for 15 to 20 (1-second) bursts, or until everything is finely chopped.

Nutrition: Calories: 106Total Fat: 11gTotal Carbs: 1gSugar: 1gFiber: 1gProtein: 2gSodium: 120mg

117) *Mushroom And Cauliflower Rice*

Preparation Time: **Cooking Time: 15 Minutes**   **Servings:6**

Ingredients:

- 1½ cups cauliflower rice
- 2 tablespoons olive oil
- 4 ounces wild mushrooms, roughly chopped
- 3 shallots, chopped

- 8 ounces cremini mushrooms, roughly chopped
- 2 cups veggie stock
- A pinch of salt and black pepper
- 2 tablespoons chopped cilantro

Directions:

⇒ Heat up a pot with the oil over medium heat and add the cauliflower rice and shallots.

⇒ Stir and cook for 5 minutes.

⇒ Add stock, cremini mushrooms and wild mushrooms, then stir and cook for 10 minutes more.

⇒ Add the parsley, salt and pepper and mix.

⇒ Divide between plates and serve.

Nutrition: Calories 189Fat 3g - Fiber 4gCarbs 9g - Protein 8g

118) *Cabbage Slaw With Cashew Dressing*

Preparation Time: **Cooking Time: 0 Minutes**   **Servings:6**

Ingredients:

- Salad:
- 2 carrots, grated
- 1 large head green or red cabbage, sliced thin
- Dressing:
- 1 cup cashews, soaked in water for at least 4 hours, drained

- ¼ cup freshly squeezed lemon juice
- ¾ teaspoon sea salt
- ½ cup water

Directions:

⇒ Combine the carrots and cabbage in a large serving bowl. Toss to combine well.

⇒ Put the ingredients for the dressing in a food processor, then pulse until creamy and smooth.

⇒ Dress the salad, then refrigerate for at least 1 hour before serving.

Nutrition: calories: 208 ; fat: 11.0g ; protein: 7.0g ; carbs: 25.0g ; fiber: 8.0g ; sugars: 4.0g ; sodium: 394mg

119) *Basic Brown Rice*

Preparation Time: **Cooking Time: 55 Minutes**   **Servings:2**

Ingredients:

- 1 cup of brown rice
- 2½ cups water

- ½ teaspoon salt

Directions:

⇒ Mix the rice, water, plus salt in a medium saucepan. Simmer, uncovered, over medium-high heat.

⇒ Set the heat to low, cover, then simmer within 45 minutes. Do not stir the rice during cooking.

⇒ When no liquid remains, remove the pan from the heat and set it aside to cool for 10 minutes.

⇒ Fluff the rice gently using a fork to avoid sticking.

Nutrition: Calories 138 Total Fat: 1g Saturated Fat: 0g Protein: 3g Total Carbohydrates: 29g Fiber: 1g Sugar: 0g Cholesterol: 0mg

Chapter 8: Anti-Inflammatory Meal Plan for Men

Day 1

1) Carrot Rice With Scrambled Eggs| Calories 230

17) Bean Shawarma Salad| Calories 173

89) Rice Pudding | Calories 170

49) Roast Chicken Dal| Calories 307

102) Garlic Aioli | Calories 169

Day 3

6) Hot Honey Porridge | Calories 172

34) Black Bean Tortilla Wrap | Calories 203

84) Turmeric Bars | Calories 410

65) Balsamic Roast Chicken | Calories 587

107) Zoodle Bolognese | Calories 457

Day 5

15) Power Protein Porridge | Calories 572

28) Brisket With Blue Cheese | Calories 397

87) Piquillo Peppers With Cheese | Calories 274

69) Pork With Thyme Sweet Potatoes | Calories 210

118) Cabbage Slaw With Cashew Dressing | Calories 208

Day 7

7) Breakfast Salad | Calories 188

25) Easy Salmon Salad | Calories 553

90) Lemony Steamed Asparagus | Calories 13

62) Chicken With Broccoli | Calories 300

100) Caesar Dressing | Calories 167

Day 2

5) Gingered Carrot & Coconut Muffins | Calories 352

23) Barbecued Ocean Trout With Garlic And Parsley Dressing | Calories 170

81) Cereal Mix | Calories 199

78) Chicken And Brussels Sprouts | Calories 200

110) Green Beans With Nuts | Calories 285

Day 4

11) Pumpkin & Banana Waffles | Calories 357

40) Leek, Chicken, And Spinach Soup | Calories 256

98) Peppers Avocado Salsa | Calories 304

52) Five-spice Roasted Duck Breasts | Calories 152

115) Peanut Sauce | Calories 143

Day 6

13) Creamy Parmesan Risotto With Mushroom And Cauliflower | Calories 179

37) Valencia Salad | Calories 238

95) Orange And Blackberry Cream | Calories 110

57) Pork With Chili Zucchinis And Tomatoes | Calories 300

114) Herbed Green Beans | Calories 66.2

Chapter 9: Conclusion

I hope this cookbook has allowed you to broaden your vision of all the possibilities you have at your fingertips to have a healthy life and leave behind the discomfort caused by inflammation.

I hope it is the first step in a new lifestyle that will allow you to enjoy your day-to-day life with more planning and significantly improve your quality of life, whether you are an office worker or an athlete, whether you live alone or with your family.

Remember that mealtime is a time to connect with yourself and become aware that what we eat and how we do it really says a lot about us and the way we take care of our body, the only one we will have for life.

If this cookbook has improved your life, remember to share it with your family, friends and colleagues, because sometimes a word is enough to change the lives of those around us for the better.

Keep in mind that if at this moment you do not give yourself the opportunity to start having a healthy diet, later will come the time of illness and negative consequences for your lack of care, so a healthy diet should not be a fad or something momentary but forever.

My most sincere good wishes, and may each recipe that you discovered here be a great experience of life and satisfy your palate.

CPSIA information can be obtained
at www.ICGtesting.com
Printed in the USA
LVHW020806160621
690358LV00012B/1916

9 781803 214801